Hands-on Mosaic

T
TRAFALGAR SQUARE
North Pomfret, Vermont

First published in the United States of America
in 2014 by
Trafalgar Square Books
North Pomfret, Vermont 05053

Originally published in French as *La Mosaïque*.

Copyright © 2012 Éditions de Saxe (www.edisaxe.com)
English translation © 2014 Trafalgar Square Books

ISBN: 978-1-57076-699-2

Library of Congress Control Number: 2014952241

Translation by Elizabeth Gray
Managing Editor: Viviane Rousset
Associate Editor: Corinne Vignane
Editorial Assistants: Béatriz Millerat, Agathe Béon
Designs: various
Photography: Magic World, Dussouillez-Mateo Studio
Interior design and illustrations: Anne Roule

Printed in China

10 9 8 7 6 5 4 3 2 1

Contents

Materials and Supplies

Materials and supplies

The tools used in mosaic are fairly simple, and once you have acquired them they may be used over and over. They are sold in craft stores and on the internet.

Materials and tools

Mosaic

Briare ceramic

Squares of 1 in / 2.5 cm to a side. Easy to work with, frost- and wear-resistant. 100 g = 20 pieces, which will cover an area approximately 5 in / 13 cm to a side.

Stone

Squares of ¾ in / 2 cm to a side; matte surface. Used to create an "antique" effect. 100 g = 30 pieces, which will cover an area approximately 5 in / 13 cm to a side.

Iridescent glass tile

Squares of ¾ in / 2 cm to a side. Smooth on the front side and grooved on the back. 100 g = 30 pieces, which will cover an area approximately 5 in / 13 cm to a side.

Transparent glass tile

Squares of ¾ in / 2 cm to a side. 100 g = 30 pieces, which will cover an area approximately 5 in / 13 cm to a side.

Ceramic pebble tiles

Striking for their unique shape and their color, these tiles are used uncut.

Glass pebbles or beads

Used in a mosaic piece to provide texture and create relief. Do not cut.

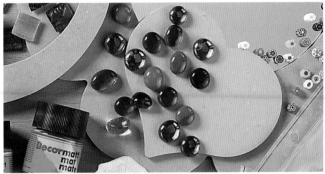

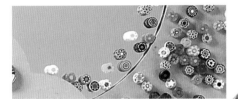

There are many other materials you can use, including Italian millefiori glass, glass rods, and tumbled pebbles. If you want to make really decorative and unique mosaics, don't hesitate to mix classic materials with whatever else you might have available—seashells, beads, buttons, small pieces of mirror...

Tools

- Tile nipper: A type of cutting pliers, so you can cut your tile as needed to give the desired shape using the edges of the jaws
- Craft tweezers: A gripping tool, so you can hold and position very small pieces of tile on the surface you're mosaicking
- Potters' rib: A handheld scraper in rubber or wood, so you can easily spread or scrape mosaic grout
- Carbon paper
- Pencil
- Felt-tipped pen
- Pliers
- Sponge
- Soft cloth
- White vinegar
- Small container for mixing grout
- Spoon
- Sandpaper, medium grit

Tips

Craft tweezers can be replaced by ordinary bathroom tweezers. The potters' rib can be replaced by a piece of cardboard, 2 x 2³/₄ in / 5 x 7 cm, bent slightly with the hands.

Adhesives, grouts, and colors

Mosaic glue in a small can

Usable on all wood, medium-density fiberboard (MDF), and polystyrene surfaces. Allows repositioning of tiles for 5 to 10 minutes. Odorless; translucent when dry.

Glass mosaic glue

Used for work involving glass tile.

Powder grout

Used to fill the spaces between tiles once they're glued in place.

Multi-surface acrylic paint

Allows for painting of surfaces or of grout.

Multi-surface varnish

Allows for a beautiful finish and protects the work. Can be matte, semi-glossy, or glossy.

Surfaces

Tile can be glued to any surface material—glass, wood, cardboard, MDF, polystyrene, metal, terracotta, plastic, canvas...

Precut fiberboard in a variety of shapes (animals, mirror frames, picture frames, figures, flowers, and others...) is commercially available in craft and hobby stores, and makes an ideal base for mosaic. Don't hesitate to use it. Fiberboard mosaics can also be mounted in a frame to create decorative and original works of art.

Preparing varnished wood

Sand the surface with medium grit sandpaper to roughen it. Remove dust from the surface with a damp rag. Cover with 2 coats of paint.

Preparing painted wood

Wash with soap to degrease, and cover with 2 coats of paint.

Preparing rusty metal

Clean with sandpaper, dust thoroughly, and then use an anti-rust metal paint.

Preparing metal, plastic, or ceramic

Degrease with soap. Lay tesserae directly onto the surface, or apply a smooth-surface primer before painting.

Preparing painted pasteboard

Sand lightly and cover with 2 coats of paint.

No matter what surface you're using, suitable primers are commercially available in craft stores that will permit the application of acrylic paint.

Tips
Mosaic is an ideal technique to give new life to objects that are past their prime. Look around in closets and attics for old mirrors, picture frames, lamp bases, clay pots, candle holders, boxes, or small articles of furniture... and you're sure to find something that will inspire you.

Technique

Mosaic should be done on a protected table, and in a room with flooring that is uncarpeted and easy to clean.

Stage 1
Designing a motif

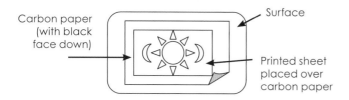

In mosaic design, geometric patterns are often used for their simplicity, but it's possible to lay out more complicated designs—without needing to know how to draw.

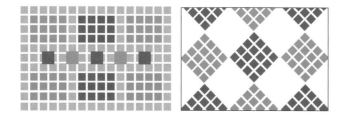

Carbon paper technique

Photocopy or print the motif you want to mosaic on a sheet of paper, resizing the image as desired. Put a sheet of carbon paper in between the printed sheet and your chosen surface.

Hold everything in place with a few pieces of tape. With a ballpoint pen or hard-leaded pencil, trace each part of the pattern carefully.

Carbon paper (with black face down) → [diagram] ← Surface

Printed sheet placed over carbon paper

How many tiles?

The number of tiles you'll need depends on the size of the surface you intend to cover and the size of the tesserae you're using.

On the surface you've chosen, use pencil to mark the borders of the different portions of your mosaic design. Make a rough estimate of the area you will be covering with your tesserae, and make sure you have extra, in case you end up discarding a few during the cutting process.

How to place them

In mosaic, it's preferable to place tesserae irregularly or at angles to each other, to avoid a certain look of heaviness.

Irregular placement gives a feeling of dynamism, of movement, and can highlight the design.

  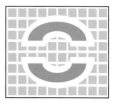

Dynamism
Place tesserae pointing in any direction.

Movement
Follow the contours of the design.

Highlight
Place a border around the main pattern and then fill in the remaining space.

How to choose colors

In mosaic, there are no rules—choose colors that appeal to your personal taste.

However, a good selection of colors can greatly enhance a piece of mosaic. Play with contrasts, and experiment with matching "warm" colors (red, orange, yellow) with "cool" colors (violet, blue, green).

Think about your paint before painting the portions of your surface or object that will not be covered by your mosaic. Below are some tips for achieving certain colors with acrylics:

turquoise:
blue + light green + white

violet:
blue + carmine red

fuchsia:
white + a
touch of red +
a small touch
of blue

lime green:
green + yellow

brown:
red + yellow
+ a touch of
blue

Stage 2
Cutting tiles

For cutting, a tile nipper is indispensable.

• For straight cuts

Place the jaws of the tile nipper where you want to make the cut, with the tile nipper positioned over ⅓ of the length of the tile. Squeeze the tile nipper: a square tile will crack into two equally-sized rectangles. The tile nipper's jaws need to be straight—parallel to the edges of the tile—in order for the resulting break to be equally straight.

In the same manner, cut each rectangle in two if you want to create smaller squares (see photo at top left). If your surface includes rounded contours, trimming squares into narrow trapezoids will help with fit.

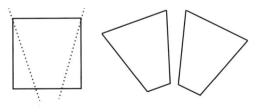

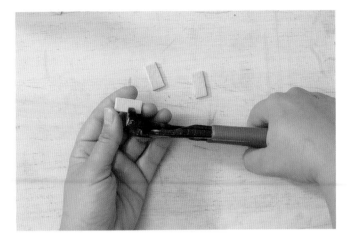

• For irregular cuts

Place the jaws of the tile nipper on a line that's not parallel to the edges of the tile, and cut.
As previously, position the tile nipper over about ⅓ of the length of the tile.

Don't hesitate to cut several pieces in a row so you can choose whichever turns out the best.
For a more precise cut on ceramic tiles, place the tile on the pattern and trace the cut you want to make with a felt-tipped marker. Don't use a marker on tiles that are matte or made of stone.
With the edges of the tile nipper, clip a bit at a time, following the line you traced with the marker.

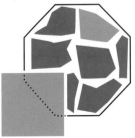

Stage 3
Gluing tile

Before you start, sort the various colors of tile you plan to use for your project onto paper plates.

Next, place some of the tesserae on your chosen surface, without any glue, to give yourself a good idea of how the final mosaic will look and to make sure you are pleased with your color choices.

Always start by gluing down the tesserae that will be at the edges of your surface or object. If you're decorating a mirror or picture frame, start with the inner and outer borders. Next lay out the major motifs, if any, and then finish with the remaining space.

Space your tesserae at regular, even, narrow intervals. If the spacing is too wide or irregular, the end result will look unbalanced and unfinished.

Either spread the mosaic glue directly on the part of the surface you're going to cover next, or put a small amount of glue on the back of each tessera before you place it.

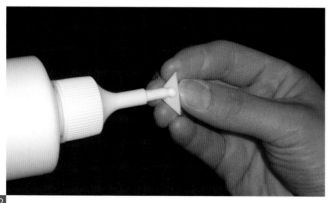

Don't step away in the middle of a project if it means you'll be leaving glue to dry on the surface without placing any tesserae. If you're interrupted partway through, wipe any excess glue off your surface with an old rag or a paper towel.

Place the tesserae on the surface where you've spread some of the glue, spacing them at regular intervals. Press lightly for best adhesion.

Repeat, alternately spreading more glue and placing tesserae until you've covered the surface as desired. Use craft tweezers—or regular bathroom tweezers—to place smaller pieces with precision.

Stage 4
Grout and finishing
◆ ● ◆ ● ◆ ● ◆ ● ◆ ● ◆

Grout is necessary as long as there is any space at all between tesserae. It allows you to fill the gaps between neighboring tesserae, protecting your work and giving it a clean, appealing look.

Cleaning off excess grout
Leave the grout to dry for at least 5 minutes, and then wipe the surface of the mosaic with a rag or a paper towel. After 30 minutes, rub a soft cloth gently over the mosaic.
Let dry for another 2 to 4 days, and then polish the mosaic thoroughly with a rag dipped in white vinegar.

Preparing grout
In a container (a bowl or jar), combine grout powder with just enough water to produce a mixture with the approximate consistency of toothpaste. Use a small spoon to stir.

Finishing
Sand the edges of the surface with medium-grit sandpaper to smooth them.
You may want to apply a full coat of varnish if the object you have mosaicked is intended for outdoor use, or will be stored or used in a humid location. The choice of whether to varnish your completed piece is up to you.

Applying grout
Apply the grout uniformly over the mosaic.
Use a potters' rib—or a small piece of cardboard—to spread the grout, and to make sure it fills the spaces between tesserae fully.
Use your fingers to fill any lingering gaps and to make sure the grout follows any unusual contours of your surface or object.

Tips
Grout can be tinted with acrylic paint. If the grout cracks or shrinks as it dries, put a little more grout over the first layer once it has dried fully.

Variation: full-sized tile mosaic

Technique

Cutting a full-sized tile into large squares

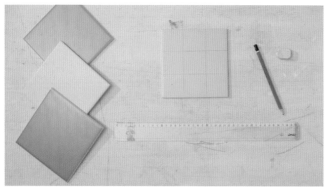

1 Mark the lines you want to cut with pencil.

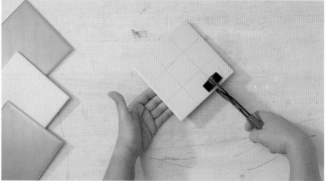

3 Position the tile cutter with the blade under the line, and squeeze. This will break the tile along the score you created.

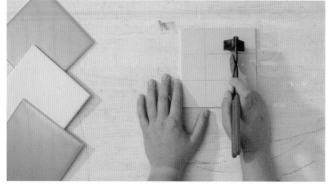

2 Place the scoring wheel of a tile cutter on one of the lines and roll the cutter along it, exerting steady pressure to score the tile.

4 Repeat with each line you marked on the tile to divide the full-sized tile into squares. Use these larger squares just like smaller tiles.

Cutting a full-sized tile into small squares

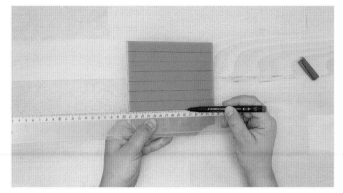

1 With the help of a ruler and permanent marker, measure out and trace lines such that the tile will be cut into squares ⅝ in / 1.5 cm to a side.

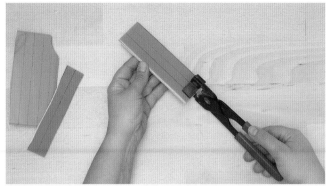

3 Position the tile cutter with the blade under the line, and squeeze. This will break the tile into 2 pieces along the score you created. Divide each of these pieces into 2 the same way. Repeat for each piece, always cutting along a line that is as close to the center of the piece as possible, until you have long rectangles ⅝ in / 1.5 cm wide.

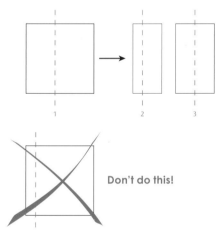

Don't do this!

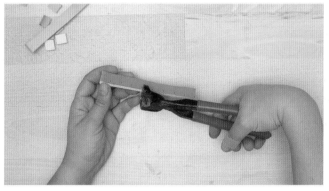

4 To cut each long rectangle into squares, position your tile nippers on one of the lines so that the jaws cover about ⅓ of the width of the rectangle. Squeeze. Repeat with each of the remaining lines you marked on the tile, always cutting along a line that is as close to the center of the piece as possible, until you have squares ⅝ in / 1.5 cm to a side.

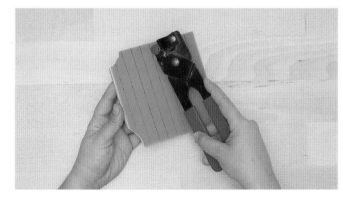

2 Run the scoring wheel of a tile cutter along one of the lines, exerting steady pressure to score the tile. The first line you cut along needs to be somewhere near the middle of the tile.

In the kitchen

✲ ✲ ✲ ✲ ✲ ✲ ✲ ✲ ✲ ✲ ✲ ✲ ✲

materials

* ✤ Tile nippers
* ✤ Craft tweezers
* ✤ Potters' rib
* ✤ Spoon
* ✤ Brush
* ✤ Pencil
* ✤ Marker
* ✤ Small jar
* ✤ Dry cloth
* ✤ White vinegar

Wine box

✲ ✲ ✲ ✲ ✲ ✲ ✲ ✲ ✲ ✲ ✲ ✲ ✲ ✲

Supplies
• Briare ceramic tile: pale blue, 100 g (20 pieces)
• Ceramic pebble tiles: turquoise, 2 large, 4 medium, and 8 small tiles
• Grout powder

Surface
• 1 wooden wine box

How to do it

Cutting and gluing the tile
Divide each Briare ceramic tile into 3 pieces, cutting irregularly (technique on page 11).
Glue these tesserae and the pebble tiles (technique on page 12), starting with the main cylinder of the wine box and continuing onto the top and bottom.
To keep the tesserae from sliding around on the curved surface while you're working, do a little bit at a time, stopping to give the glue a chance to dry.
Let dry thoroughly before applying grout.

Grout and finishing
Follow the instructions on page 13.

Stool

Supplies
• Briare ceramic tile: pale blue, 150 g (30 pieces); pale green, 100 g (20 pieces); beige, 500 g (100 pieces)
• Ceramic pebble tiles: turquoise, 2 very large, 4 large, 6 medium, and 10 small tiles
• Grout powder

Surface
• 1 wooden stool

How to do it

Preparing the surface
If the stool is made of unfinished wood, it can be painted with acrylic paint after the mosaic is complete, as long as you're careful not to get any paint on the tile.
On the other hand, if the stool is already painted, the paint needs to be roughened with steel wool everywhere you'll be gluing tile, and sanded with medium-grit sandpaper everywhere else before you start working on your mosaic.

Cutting and gluing the tile
Divide the blue and green Briare ceramic tiles into 3 pieces, cutting irregularly (technique on page 11). Cut some of the beige tile the same way. Cut the remainder into fourths with straight cuts (technique on page 11) so they will fit around the edge of the seat.
Begin gluing the tesserae, starting with the edge and then proceeding to glue the irregular pieces and the pebble tiles across the surface of the seat. Consider placing the tesserae so that they cover the edges of the tesserae you laid first.

Grout and finishing
Follow the instructions on page 13.

Tray

✳ ✳ ✳ ✳ ✳ ✳ ✳

Supplies
• Briare enamel tile: pale blue, 150 g (30 pieces); pale green, 150 g (30 pieces); beige, 200 g (40 pieces)
• Ceramic pebble tiles: turquoise, 2 very large, 4 large, 8 medium, and 6 small tiles
• Grout powder

Surface
• 1 wooden tray, 15¾ x 22⅞ in / 40 x 58 cm

How to do it

Preparing the surface
If you buy a plain tray from a craft store, it will probably be unfinished wood, but it's entirely possible to paint it before laying your mosaic.

Cutting and gluing the tile
Divide the Briare ceramic tiles into 3 pieces, cutting irregularly (technique on page 11).
Begin gluing beige tesserae (technique on page 12) along the edge of the tray's surface, and then glue the pebble tiles. Then fill in the remainder of the tray's surface, laying pieces of each color in no particular order. (At this point, you will probably have fewer pieces of beige left, relative to the other colors—try to space these evenly but randomly across the surface of the tray.)
Let dry thoroughly.

Grout and finishing
Follow the instructions on page 13.

To-do slate

✹ ✹ ✹ ✹ ✹ ✹ ✹ ✹ ✹ ✹ ✹ ✹

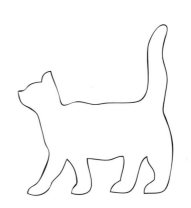

Supplies
- Briare ceramic tile: dark green, 50 g (10 pieces); turquoise, 50 g (10 pieces); light green, 50 g (10 pieces); very light green, 50 g (10 pieces); red, 10 g (2 pieces); yellow, 20 g (4 pieces); white, 5 g (1 piece)
- 1 ceramic cat, white
- 1 ceramic butterfly, red

Surface
- 1 slate with a 2 in / 5 cm-wide wooden frame

How to do it

Cutting the tile
This mosaic requires patience, time, and a helping hand. You may want to have some extra tiles on hand.

- **Flower centers**

Cut the white tile into 9 squares (technique on page 11). On 3 of the squares, trace circles with a marker, and then cut them out by trimming a bit at a time (technique on page 11).

- **Flower petals**

Cut the red and yellow tiles into 3 long rectangles each, and then cut each long rectangle in half to obtain 6 smaller rectangles. Draw an oval on each of these rectangles with the marker. Trim the rectangles down to the lines with tile nippers.

- **Grass**

Cut the rest of the tiles into narrow rectangles, and then trim them into irregular, tapering waves with tile nippers.

Gluing the tile
This mosaic doesn't use any grout, so it's important to put only a little glue on each piece—try to avoid having any excess that will squeeze out when you press the pieces into place.

Start by gluing down the centers of the flowers in about the middle of the frame, and then glue the petals around them.

Glue the grass around the flowers. Make sure all the grass is placed so that it points the same direction, tapering ends up, to preserve the illusion of movement. Let dry thoroughly.

Finishing
Finish by gluing the cat at the bottom of the slate and the butterfly on the righthand side of the frame.

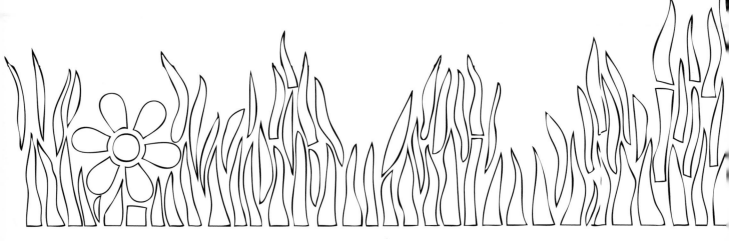

- Cream
- Eggs
- Bacon
- Puff pastry
- Cheese
- Ham

A hot dinner

✲ ✲ ✲ ✲ ✲ ✲ ✲ ✲ ✲ ✲ ✲ ✲

Supplies
• Micro-mosaic tiles, ³⁄₁₆ in / 5 mm: orange, 40 g; beige, 40 g; brown, 40 g; black, 30 g; ivory, 10 g
• Micro-mosaic tiles, ⅛ in / 3 mm: orange, 20 g; brown, 20 g; black, 10 g
• Acrylic paint, sienna
• Grout powder

Surfaces
• 1 fiberboard dinner tray, 15¾ x 11¾ in / 40 x 30 cm
• 1 fiberboard napkin ring, shaped like a sun
• 1 fiberboard egg cup
• 1 fiberboard candle holder, shaped like a sun

Dinner tray

✲ ✲ ✲ ✲ ✲ ✲ ✲ ✲ ✲ ✲

How to do it

Preparing the surface
The tray is mosaicked with ³⁄₁₆ in / 5 mm tiles only.
With a pencil, trace a line about ⅝ in / 1.5 cm from the edges of the long sides of the tray, and about 2⅛ in / 5.5 cm from the edges of the short sides of the tray.
Connect these lines to each other with beveled corners, not square corners.

Gluing the tile
Glue orange tile around the outer edge of the entire tray, and just to the outside of the lines you drew parallel to the short sides of the tray. Glue brown tile around the inside edges of the lines you drew, all the way around the tray.
Glue black tiles in the middle of the space available along the short sides of the tray, creating a wavelike shape. Then glue ivory tiles and black tiles into small "flowers"—three in the curves of your waves and one in each corner—with black centers and 4 ivory "petals" apiece.

Grout and finishing
Fill in the corners with orange tile and the sides with beige (see photo for guidance). Try to space your tiles as evenly as possible. Follow the instructions on page 13 for applying grout. Let dry. Cover the mosaicked area so it is protected, and then paint the tray sienna with the acrylic paint.

Egg cup

How to do it

Preparing the surface

With a pencil, trace lines to mark out the spaces occupied by the various colors (see photo for guidance). The line you trace for the brown tiles should be around the middle of the cup.

Gluing the tile

Glue a row of ³/₁₆ in / 5 mm brown tiles on the middle line, placing them diagonally. Surround this row on either side with rows of beige tiles—also diagonally placed, and aligned so that they only touch corners with the brown row (see photo for guidance). Fill in the spaces with ⅛ in / 3 mm brown tile.

Glue one row of ⅛ in / 3 mm brown tiles to the base of the egg cup. Fill in the remaining space on the body of the cup with diagonally placed ⅛ in / 3 mm orange tile. On a line around the middle of the base, glue a row of ⅛ in / 3 mm black tiles, placing them diagonally. Finish with a row of ⅛ in / 3 mm orange tiles around the upper part of the base.

Grout and finishing

Follow the instructions on page 13 for applying grout. Let dry. Cover the mosaicked area so it is protected, and then paint the remaining visible surface of the cup sienna with the acrylic paint.

Candle holder

How to do it

The candle holder is mosaicked with ³/₁₆ in / 5 mm tiles only.

Gluing the tile

Start by gluing a ring of black tiles around the inside edge of the candle holder. Then glue a row of beige tile outside the ring of black, placing them diagonally, and then place another ring of black tiles.

Fill in the sun's "rays," alternating a ray of brown tiles with a ray of beige tiles.

Grout and finishing

Follow the instructions on page 13 for applying grout. Let dry. Cover the mosaicked area so it is protected, and then paint the visible sides of the candle holder sienna with the acrylic paint.

Napkin ring

How to do it

Gluing the tile

Start by gluing ³/₁₆ in / 5 mm black tile around the inside edge of the napkin ring.

Then place black tiles in the middle of each of the napkin ring's "rays," varying size (see photo for guidance). Glue ³/₁₆ in / 5 mm orange tile around the outside edge of the napkin ring. Then fill in the remaining space with orange tiles of both sizes. Mosaic the second face of the napkin ring the same way.

Grout and finishing

Follow the instructions on page 13 for applying grout. Let dry. Cover the mosaicked area so it is protected, and then paint the remaining visible area sienna with the acrylic paint.

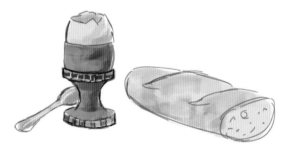

Hearts slate

✳ ✳ ✳ ✳ ✳ ✳ ✳ ✳ ✳ ✳ ✳ ✳ ✳ ✳

Supplies
• Micro-mosaic tiles, 3/16 in / 5 mm: red, 10 g; white, 10 g; pink, 10 g
• Micro-mosaic tiles, 1/8 in / 3 mm; red, 10 g; pink, 10 g
• Acrylic paint, white and red
• Grout powder

Surface
• 1 slate with a 11⅜ x 16½ in / 29 x 42 cm fiberboard frame
• 2 fiberboard hearts, 4 in / 10 cm
• 1 polystyrene heart, 2 in / 5 cm

How to do it

Preparing the surface
Paint the slate's frame red with the acrylic paint.

Cutting and gluing the tile
On the fiberboard hearts, use 3/16 in / 5 mm tiles only. Glue a row of red tiles around the outer contours of each heart (technique on page 12). Cut tiles as necessary to fit the angles (technique on page 11). Glue a row of white tiles, and then a row of pink, again cutting as necessary to fit the angles. Finish the interiors with red tile.
On the polystyrene heart, use 1/8 in / 3 mm tiles only. Glue 4 rows of red tiles to the heart, beginning at the edge and working inward, and cover the rest of the surface with pink. Try to space your tiles as evenly as possible.

Grout and finishing
Follow the instructions on page 13 for applying grout. Let dry.
Paint the remaining visible area of the hearts white with the acrylic paint.
Glue the hearts to the frame of the slate, along the lines of what is shown in the photo.

- milk, yeast
eggs, vanilla
flour

- Marie
tomorrow 4 pm

In the bathroom

■ ● ■ ● ■ ● ■ ● ■ ● ■ ● ■ ● ■ ● ■ ● ■ ● ■

Tissue box

■ ● ■ ● ■ ● ■ ● ■ ● ■ ● ■ ● ■ ● ■ ● ■ ● ■ ●

Supplies
• Briare ceramic tile: dark blue, 80 g (16 pieces); blue-black, 80 g (16 pieces)
• Ceramic pebble tiles: light blue, 1 very large, 4 large, 11 medium, and 12 small tiles
• Acrylic paint, sea-blue and black
• Grout powder
• Varnish

Surface
• 1 wooden tissue box, unfinished

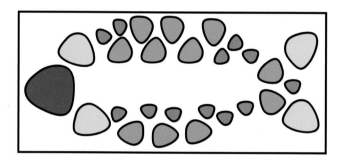

How to do it

Cutting and gluing the tile
With a pencil, trace the shape of a fish on the top of the tissue box.
Take 4 tiles (2 dark blue, 2 blue-black), and use the marker to draw a rounded corner (see diagram below for guidance). With tile nippers, trim these tiles along the lines.

At each corner of the top of the box, glue one of the rounded-off tiles.

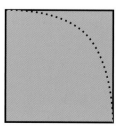

Next, cut 6 dark blue tiles and 6 blue-black tiles into 2 equal pieces each. Glue the resulting rectangles along the edge of the top of the box, alternating colors. Glue the ceramic pebble tiles, following the diagram above.
Red: very large
Yellow: large
Green: medium
Purple: small
Fill in the rest of the surface with irregularly-cut pieces (technique on page 11) of the remaining dark blue and blue-black tiles. Let dry.

Grout and finishing
Follow the instructions on page 13 for applying grout. For the fish, tint the grout with blue paint, and add a little extra powder to the paste to make it thicker. Carefully fill in all the spaces.
For the rest of the surface, tint the grout with blue paint and a touch of black. Be careful not to spill any on the fish.
Paint the remaining surface of the box blue with the acrylic paint. Varnish the box.

Fish

■●■●■●■●■●■

Supplies
- Ceramic pebble tiles: light blue, 1 medium and
- 33 small tiles; dark blue, 7 medium and 32 small tiles
- 1 glass pebble, clear
- Acrylic paint, white
- Grout powder

Surface
- 1 fiberboard fish

How to do it

Gluing the tile
Begin by gluing the light blue pebble tiles around the outside edge of the fish, and then glue the glass pebble for the fish's eye.
Cover the rest of the surface with the dark blue pebble tiles, placing the medium tiles first and then filling in the remaining area with the small tiles.
Let dry.

Grout and finishing
Add a little extra powder to the grout to make it thicker, and follow the instructions on page 13. Paint the remaining visible fiberboard white with the acrylic paint.

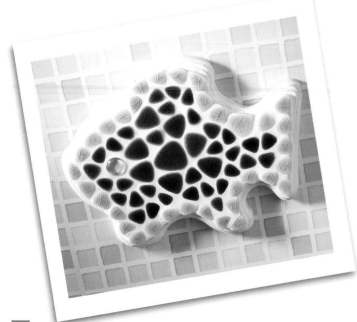

Candle holder

■●■●■●■●■●■●■○●

Supplies
- Glass tile, ¾ in / 2 cm: shades of blue, 160 g (53 pieces)
- 23 glass pebbles, blue
- 5 plastic shells, blue
- Acrylic paint, white and light blue
- Grout powder

Surface
1 square wooden candle tray, unfinished, 10⅝ x 10⅝ in / 27 x 27 cm

How to do it

Preparing the surface
Start by painting the inside and outside of the candle tray blue with the acrylic paint (with the exception of the flat area you're going to mosaic), and then paint the edges white.

Gluing the tile
Glue the plastic shells on 2 opposing corners of the tray (see photo for guidance) with mosaic glue.
Glue the glass tile (technique on page 12) around the outer edge of the tray surface, varying colors as you go, and then glue the glass pebbles in groups of 3 or 5. Fill any remaining empty space around the inner edge with more glass tile.
Let dry.

Grout and finishing
Add a little extra powder to the grout to make it thicker, and follow the instructions on page 13.
Let dry 1 hour, and then take a sharp instrument (scissors or a knife) and carefully scratch away any excess grout in the grooves of the shells or around the bases of the glass pebbles.

Tissue box
■●■●■●■●■●■●□

Supplies
• Briare ceramic tile: shades of white and off-white, 600 g (117 pieces)
• Ceramic pebble tiles: white, 2 very large, 6 large, 12 medium, and 10 small tiles
• Grout powder

Surface
• 1 wooden tissue box

How to do it

Cutting and gluing the tile
Cut some of the square ceramic tiles into about 3 irregular pieces (technique on page 11).
Prepare another set of tiles by cutting them into quarters, making smaller equally-sized squares (technique on page 11). These will border the top edge of the box.
Cut a few remaining tiles into very narrow rectangles, sized to fit the lip at the short sides of the top of the box.
Start by gluing the pebble tiles to all 4 sides and the top of the box; fill in the remaining space with the irregularly-cut tesserae.
Glue the narrowly-cut tesserae along the lip at the top of the box.
Finish by filling in the remaining space on the top of the box, and then glue the small square tesserae along the top edge.
Let dry.

Grout and finishing
Follow the instructions on page 13.

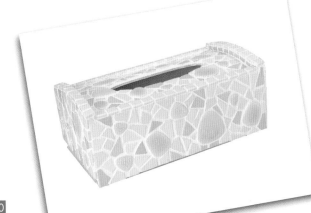

Small bowl
■●■●■●■●■●■●□

Supplies
• Speckled stone tile, ¾ in / 2 cm: beige, 50 g (10 pieces); light brown, 50 g (10 pieces)
• Grout powder

Surface
• 1 terra cotta plant saucer, 4 in / 10 cm diameter

How to do it

Cutting and gluing the tile
Cut 7 of the beige tiles into quarters, all 10 of the light brown tiles in half, and the remaining beige tiles irregularly (technique on page 11).
Start by gluing the small beige squares around the upper edge of the plant saucer, about ¾ in / 2 cm apart. Turn the saucer as you work to ensure that the tesserae are well aligned.
Glue the light brown rectangles around the inside lip of the saucer.
Trim the remaining beige squares, beveling two corners so that the tesserae are trapezoidal, and then glue them in the spaces you left between the squares you already glued to the saucer's edge.
In the remaining space in the middle of the saucer, glue the irregularly-cut tesserae.

Grout and finishing
Follow the instructions on page 13.

Mirror

■●■●■●■●■●■

Supplies
• Ceramic tiles in specialty shapes: blue, 55 triangles and 4 stars
• 12 gilt glass beads

Surface
• 1 mirror with a large wooden frame

How to do it

Gluing the tile
Glue the various pieces, taking care not to mark up the wood. File or sand down tiles at the edge of the frame.

Grout and finishing
This mosaic doesn't use any grout.

Cotton jar

■●■●■●■●■●■●■●■

Supplies
• Round Venetian smalti tiles: shades of blue, 140 g (28 pieces)

Surface
• 1 square ceramic container

How to do it

Gluing the tile
Place the tiles freehand, in whatever arrangement the container and colors inspire.

Grout and finishing
This mosaic doesn't use any grout.

Soap dish

■●■●■●■●■●■●■●■●■

Supplies
• Briare ceramic tile: shades of blue, 60 g (12 pieces)
• Ceramic tiles in specialty shapes: yellow, ocean-themed (6 total)
• Acrylic paint, blue
• Grout powder

Surface
• 1 square ceramic soap dish

How to do it

Gluing the tile
On the inside bottom of the soap dish, glue the square ceramic tiles, varying colors and cutting tiles as necessary to fit.
On the outside of the soap dish, glue the ocean-themed tiles. Take care not to use too much glue, or you may end up smearing some on areas that will not be covered up—if this happens, clean off the excess glue immediately. Let dry.

Grout and finishing
Follow the instructions on page 13 for applying grout. Tint the grout with the blue paint before application.

Toothpaste holder

■●■●■●■●■●■●■●■●■●■

Supplies
• Square Venetian smalti tiles, ⅜ in / 1 cm: shades of blue, 200 g (144 pieces)

Surface
• 1 square ceramic container

How to do it

Gluing the tile
Glue the tiles to each face of the container in turn, without leaving space between. You may want to give this kind of placement a try without glue first. Begin at the center and work your way outward over the remaining area, varying colors.

Grout and finishing
This mosaic doesn't use any grout.

Island ambiance

■●■●■●■●■●■●■●■●■●■●■

Supplies
• Briare ceramic tile: yellow, 300 g (60 pieces); dark blue, 150 g (30 pieces); light blue, 150 g (30 pieces)
• 1 glass pebble, white
• Acrylic paint, white
• Grout powder

Surface
• 1 mirror with a fiberboard frame in the shape of a fish

How to do it

Preparing the surface
Remove the mirror from the frame and put it safely out of the way.
Paint the edges of the frame white with the acrylic paint.
Trace lines on the frame to indicate where you will place each color (see photo for guidance).

Cutting and gluing the tile
Glue the white glass pebble in place for the fish's eye.
Cut some of the the blue tiles of both shades into rectangles of different sizes, and glue them along the lines you traced for the fish's stripes.
Cut the yellow tiles into irregular pieces (technique on page 11), and fill in the remaining space between the stripes. Remember to space your tesserae as evenly as possible (technique on page 12).
For the mouth, cut some of the light blue tiles into irregular pieces (technique on page 11), and glue them down.
For the fish's fins, cut blue tiles of both shades into irregular slivers with tile nippers. This kind of cutting takes a little time to master, so it may be a good idea to practice on some spare tiles. Glue them down, following the contours of the frame.

Grout and finishing
Follow the instructions on page 13.
Put the mirror back into place.

Tropical heat

■●■●■●■●■●■●■●■●■●■●■

Supplies

for the frame
• Micro-mosaic tiles, 3/16 in / 5 mm: salmon, 10 g; green, 10 g; orange, 10 g; light pink, 10 g
• 4 glass pebbles, orange

for the box
• Micro-mosaic tiles, 3/16 in / 5 mm: salmon, 10 g; orange, 10 g; light pink, 20 g
• Micro-mosaic tiles, 1/8 in / 3 mm: salmon, 10 g; green, 10 g; orange, 10 g; light pink, 10 g; light orange, 10 g
• Millefiori glass tiles: orange, 2 pieces
• Briare ceramic tile, 3/8 in / 1 cm: salmon, 2 pieces
• 1 transparent glass tile, 3/4 in / 2 cm: orange

for the bracelet
• Micro-mosaic tiles, 3/16 in / 5 mm: orange, 10 g; light pink, 10 g
• Micro-mosaic tiles, 1/8 in / 3 mm: salmon, 10 g; orange, 10 g

for the keychain
• Micro-mosaic tiles, 3/16 in / 5 mm: salmon, 10 g; green, 10 g
• 2 pieces of leather cord, 9½ in / 24 cm long: white, turquoise
• 18⅞ in/ 48 cm of nylon cord
• Seed beads, orange
• 6 larger transparent beads, orange
• 4 crimp beads
• 1 carabiner, 1⅛ in / 3 cm

for all projects
• Acrylic paint, orange and brown
• Grout powder

Surfaces

• 1 fiberboard frame with stands, 4 x 6 in / 10 x 15 cm
• 1 wooden oval-shaped box, 4⅜ in x 6 in / 11 x 15 cm
• 1 fiberboard butterfly, 2 x 2 in / 5 x 5 cm
• 1 wooden bracelet
• 1 large wooden bead, 1⅛ in / 3 cm in diameter

How to do it

Frame

Paint the edges, the stands, and the back of the frame orange with the acrylic paint, and let dry.
Glue the glass pebbles to the 4 inner corners of the frame.
Glue salmon tiles around the inside and outside edges of the frame, pink tiles around the glass pebbles, and green tiles diagonally, 3 at the top of the frame and 3 at the bottom (see photo for guidance). Glue salmon tile along the front edges of the frame stands. Fill in the remaining visible area with yellow and orange tile. Follow the instructions on page 13 for applying grout.

Box

Paint the sides of the box and the edges of the butterfly orange and the surface of the lid brown with the acrylic paint. Let dry.
For the lid, use 3/16 in / 5 mm tile. In the middle of the front side of the lid, glue the 3/4 in / 2 cm transparent glass tile. Glue 4 light pink tiles on either side. Next, glue a second column on either side: 1 orange tile, 2 salmon tiles, 1 orange tile. Glue the 3/8 in / 1 cm salmon tile next to the 2 smaller salmon tiles on either side, and then repeat the orange-salmon-orange column on the far side. Fill in above and below the 3/8 in / 1 cm salmon tile with 2 small salmon tiles (see photo for guidance). Cover the rest of the sides of the lid with light pink tile.
For the butterfly, use 1/8 in / 3 mm tile. With a pencil, mark out the various "color zones." Fill in the body of the butterfly with orange tile, outline the wings with salmon and green tile, and place the 2 millefiori tiles symmetrically, 1 in each lower wing. Fill in the remaining area with various colors, following your pencil marks. Follow the instructions on page 13 for applying grout. Glue the butterfly to the middle of the lid.

Bracelet

Paint the edges and the inside of the bracelet orange. Let dry.
Locate the center of the outside area of the bracelet, and draw a line around the middle. Glue 3/16 in / 5 mm tiles onto your line, alternating between salmon and orange. Fill in the remaining visible area with 1/8 in / 3 mm tiles, positioning them irregularly and alternating colors as desired.
Follow the instructions on page 13 for applying grout.

Keychain

Locate the center of the large wooden bead, and draw a line around the middle. Glue a row of green tiles, positioned diagonally, along your line. On either side of the green row, glue a row of salmon tiles, also positioned diagonally (see photo for guidance). Fill in the remaining visible area with salmon tile, positioned squarely.
Follow the instructions on page 13 for applying grout.
Cut the nylon cord into 2 and, for each length: Seal 1 end with a crimp bead, thread 2¾ in / 7 cm of seed beads, thread 1 or 2 larger orange beads, thread seed beads until the beaded length totals 6⅜ in / 16 cm; pass the nylon cord through the large wooden bead, through the end of the carabiner, and back through the large wooden bead; thread 1 or 2 larger orange beads, thread seed beads until you reach the end of the cord, and seal the remaining end with another crimp bead.
Pass the leather cords through the large wooden bead, through the end of the carabiner, and back through the large wooden bead.

Accessories

materials

* Tile nippers
* Craft tweezers
* Potters' rib
* Spoon
* Brush
* Pencil
* Marker
* Small jar
* Dry cloth
* White vinegar

Small tray

Supplies
• Iridescent glass tile: shades of blue, 35 g (23 pieces); shades of silver, 35 g (23 pieces)
• Grout powder, gray
• Bronze polish
• Blue oxidizer

Surface
• 1 small wooden tray, unfinished

How to do it

Gluing the tile
Glue the tile to the inner bottom surface of the tray (technique on page 12), varying colors as desired. Let dry.

Grout and finishing
Follow the instructions on page 13.
Use a brush to apply oxidizer to the tray; let dry. Apply a small amount of bronze polish with a cloth.

Decorative Mosaic

Candle holders

Supplies (for each candle holder)
- Iridescent glass tile: a mixture of bronze, brown, silver, and violet, 50 g (34 pieces)
- Grout powder, gray
- Bronze paint
- Bronze polish

Surface
2 wooden candle holders, unfinished, 2¾ x 2¾ x 4 in / 7 x 7 x 10 cm

How to do it

Gluing the tile
Glue tile around the edges of each candle holder (technique on page 12), varying colors. Place the corner tile with extra care to keep the corners square. Then glue the remaining tiles over the remaining flat area. Cut tiles in half if necessary for fit. Let dry.

Grout and finishing
Follow the instructions on page 13.
Use a brush to apply the bronze paint to any remaining visible wood. Let dry at least 15 minutes, and then apply bronze polish with a cloth.

Colorful candle holder

Supplies
- Briare ceramic tile: vivid blue, 300 g (60 pieces); yellow-green, 200 g (40 pieces)
- Grout powder

Surface
- 1 rectangular terra cotta candle holder, 2 x 2½ x 13 in long / 5 x 6.5 x 33 cm long

How to do it

Cutting and gluing the tile
Cut the tiles into squares and rectangles of various sizes (technique on page 11).
Glue them down, starting with the edges and then filling in the remaining visible space.
Let dry.

Grout and finishing
Follow the instructions on page 13.
A mosaic done on terra cotta dries quickly because the surface is porous—don't wait too long to clean off excess glue or grout.

Key box

Supplies
- Speckled stone tile, ¾ in / 2 cm: beige, 275 g (55 pieces); light brown, 275 g (55 pieces)
- 5 keys, plastic and metal
- Acrylic paint, ivory
- Grout powder
- Varnish

Surface
- 1 wooden key box

How to do it

Preparing the surface
Remove, if possible, the "door" of the key box and the key hooks. Paint the box ivory with the acrylic paint.

Cutting and gluing the tile
Cut the plastic keys into 2 or 3 pieces. Glue whole keys and pieces of keys to the inner surface of the key box. Cut the tile into irregular shapes (technique on page 11). Glue the pieces around the keys first, and then fill in the rest. Be careful to leave space to reinsert the key hooks.
Let dry.

Grout and finishing
Follow the instructions on page 13.
This project tends to look better varnished.
Put the "door" and the key hooks back in place.

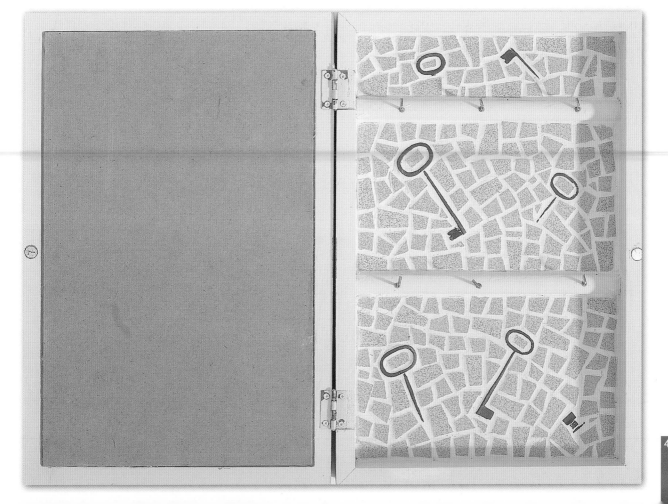

Small ceramic bowl

Supplies
- Briare ceramic tile: white, 70 g (14 pieces); beige, 35 g (7 pieces); cream, 10 g (2 pieces)
- Ceramic pebble tiles: white, 2 medium and
- 2 small tiles
- Grout powder

Surface
- 1 terra cotta plant saucer, 4 in / 10 cm diameter

How to do it

Cutting and gluing the tile
Cut 12 of the white ceramic tiles into small squares (technique on page 11), and cut the remaining tiles of all colors into irregular shapes (technique on page 11). Glue some of the small white squares (technique on page 12) around the upper edge of the saucer, about ¾ in / 2 cm apart. Turn the saucer as you work to ensure that the tesserae are well aligned. Then glue more small white squares around the inside lip of the saucer.
Trim the remaining small white squares, beveling two corners so that the tesserae are trapezoidal, and then glue them in the spaces you left between the squares you already glued to the saucer's edge.
In the remaining space in the middle of the saucer, place the ceramic pebble tiles and then the irregularly-cut tesserae, varying colors.

Grout and finishing
Follow the instructions on page 13.

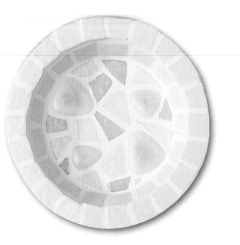

Picture frame

Supplies
- Briare ceramic tile: white, 50 g (10 pieces); beige, 150 g (30 pieces); cream, 50 g (10 pieces)
- Ceramic pebble tiles: white, 3 large, 6 medium, and 13 small tiles
- Grout powder

Surface
- 1 wooden three-part picture frame, unfinished, 7⅞ x 11¾ in in / 20 x 30 cm

How to do it

Cutting and gluing the tile
Start by cutting 20 beige tiles into 3 equal rectangles, and glue them along the edges of the frame. Cut them into even smaller pieces if necessary to fit.
Cut the rest of the square ceramic tiles into irregular shapes (technique on page 11). Glue the ceramic pebble tiles into place on the open areas of the frame, and then fill in the remaining area with the irregularly-cut tesserae. Let dry.

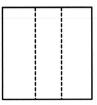

Grout and finishing
Follow the instructions on page 13.

Magnet board

Supplies
• Micro-mosaic tiles, 3/16 in / 5 mm: red, 10 g; yellow, 10 g; green, 20 g
• Micro-mosaic tiles, 1/8 in / 3 mm: white, 20 g; green, 10 g; orange, 10 g; red, 10 g; yellow, 10 g; turquoise, 10 g; light blue, 10 g; blue, 10 g; dark blue, 10 g
• 1 glass pebble, orange
• 2 rhinestones: 1 red, 1 blue
• 1 small glass pebble, blue
• 4 small glass rocks: 1 red, 1 orange, 1 green, and 1 yellow
• 1 transparent glass tile, 3/4 in / 2 cm: orange
• 2 transparent glass tiles, 3/8 in / 1 cm: 1 blue-gray, 1 aquamarine
• 3 magnets
• Acrylic paint: white and blue
• Magnetic paint
• Grout powder

Surface
• 1 fiberboard frame, 13¾ x 13¾ in / 35 x 35 cm
• 5 fiberboard shapes: 1 whale, 2 in / 5 cm; 1 fish, 2 in / 5 cm; 1 dolphin, 2 in / 5 cm; 1 starfish, 4 in / 10 cm; 1 seahorse, 4 in / 10 cm

How to do it

Preparing the surface
Paint the edges of the frame white with the acrylic paint. Apply 2 coats of magnetic paint to the interior surface of the frame. Let dry at least 2 hours, and then paint the magnetic surface blue with the acrylic paint. Paint the edges and backs of the fiberboard shapes white with the acrylic paint.

Seahorse
With a pencil, mark out the various "color zones." Glue 1 row of 3/16 in / 5 mm orange tiles around the edge of the seahorse. Cut some 3/16 in / 5 mm red, orange, and yellow tiles into 2 equal rectangles. Glue the red rectangles to the fin on the seahorse's back, the orange and some of the yellow rectangles to the seahorse's crest, and the rest of the yellow rectangles to the seahorse's snout. Fill in the remainder of the body with 3/16 in / 5 mm yellow tile, placed diagonally. Fill in any remaining uncovered areas of the surface and difficult curves with any leftover rectangles (see photo for guidance).

Starfish
Glue the orange glass pebble in the middle of the starfish. With a pencil, mark out the various "color zones." Cut some 3/16 in / 5 mm orange tiles into 2 equal rectangles, and glue some of the rectangles so that they surround the glass pebble, short sides in (see photo for guidance). Glue the rest along your pencil lines. Glue 3/16 in / 5 mm red tiles around the edges of the starfish, and then in the remaining visible area.

Dolphin
With a pencil, mark out the various "color zones." Glue the blue rhinestone in place for the dolphin's eye. Glue 1/8 in / 3 mm white tiles on the dolphin's head, 1/8 in / 3 mm dark blue tiles to the dolphin's dorsal fin and tail, and 1/8 in / 3 mm blue tiles to the remaining visible area.

Fish
With a pencil, mark out the various "color zones." Glue the red rhinestone in place for the fish's eye. Fill in the rest of the fish as desired with 1/8 in / 3 mm tiles (see photo for guidance).

Whale
With a pencil, mark out the various "color zones." Glue the small glass pebble in place for the whale's eye. Glue 1/8 in / 3 mm turquoise tiles to the whale's tail. Glue 1/8 in / 3 mm light blue tiles around the edges of the whale, and then in the remaining visible area.

Frame
Glue the glass rocks and transparent tiles in opposite corners of the frame (see photo for guidance). Glue 1/8 in / 3 mm orange, yellow, and green tiles in place first, forming coral-like shapes. Fill in the remaining visible area with 1/8 in / 3 mm white tiles, placed diagonally.

Grout and finishing
For each part, let dry and then follow the instructions on page 13 for applying grout.
Glue the seahorse and the starfish in opposite corners of the frame (see photo for guidance). Glue a magnet to the reverse of the other 3 shapes.

Fun photos

Supplies
• Micro-mosaic tiles, ³⁄₁₆ in / 5 mm, for the frame: pink, 10 g; green, 10 g; turquoise, 10 g; white, 10 g; orange, 10 g
• Micro-mosaic tiles, ⅛ in / 3 mm, for the mini clothespins: pink, 10 g; green, 10 g; turquoise, 10 g; orange, 10 g
• Acrylic paint, cream
• 4 lengths of reinforced thread, 17¾ in / 45 cm: 1 each of pink, turquoise, green, orange
• Grout powder

Surface
• 1 fiberboard frame, 13¾ x 13¾ in / 35 x 35 cm
• 16 wooden mini clothespins

How to do it

Preparing the surface
Paint the frame cream with the acrylic paint, except for the corner areas where you'll be gluing tile.

Gluing the tile
In each corner of the frame, glue white tiles so that they form a square, 3 tiles to a side. In the middle of each white square, glue 1 tile of a different color. Glue 4 additional squares along the frame on either side of each white square, each square in a different color with 1 white tile at the center (see photo for guidance). Divide the mini clothespins into groups of 4, one for each color, and glue a row of ⅛ in / 3 mm tiles to the outside surfaces of each clothespin.

Grout and finishing
Follow the instructions on page 13.
Affix the reinforced thread with small thumbtacks on the back of the frame.
Put the clothespins on the threads.

Wall art and mirrors

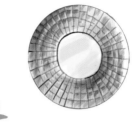

Horizontal wall mosaic

Supplies
• Glazed ceramic tile, ⅜ in / 1 cm: green, 10 g (7 pieces); shades of pink, 295 g (195 pieces)
• Acrylic paint, black
• Masking tape
• Grout powder

Surface
• 1 triangular linen canvas, mounted on a frame, 11 x 11 x 15⅜ in / 28 x 28 x 39 cm
• 1 plastic cup

How to do it

Cutting and gluing the tile
Cut the plastic cup in half with a pair of scissors, and glue it to the canvas.
Cut some salmon pink tiles to fit (technique on page 11) and glue them to the side and bottom of the cup.
Fill in the tip of the triangle with light pink tile, the upper part of the triangle with peach-pink tile, and include green tiles here and there. You will have to cut some of the tiles to fit along the diagonal lines of the canvas. Let dry.

Grout and finishing
Put the masking tape along the cup's sides and along the edges of the mosaicked areas to keep grout off the unmosaicked canvas.
Tint the grout with the acrylic paint to make it gray, and then follow the instructions on page 13.
Complete the top of the piece by gluing some tiles one by one (see photo for guidance).

Angled wall mosaic

Supplies
• Glazed ceramic tile, ⅜ in / 1 cm: burgundy, 120 g (75 pieces); shades of green, 100 g (65 pieces)
• Masking tape
• Acrylic paint, black
• Grout powder

Surface
• 1 triangular linen canvas, mounted on a frame, 11 x 11 x 15⅜ in / 28 x 28 x 39 cm
• 1 plastic cup

How to do it

Cutting and gluing the tile
Cut the cup in half with a pair of scissors and glue it to the canvas.
Cut some of the burgundy tiles into irregular shapes (technique on page 11) and glue them to the bottom of the cup. Continue gluing tiles across the front of the cup—mostly burgundy, with a few shades of green included (see photo for guidance).
Complete the piece by gluing the remaining green tiles to the canvas (see photo for guidance).

Grout and finishing
Put the masking tape along the cup's sides and along the edges of the mosaicked areas to keep grout off the unmosaicked canvas.
Tint the grout with the acrylic paint to make it gray, and then follow the instructions on page 13.

Picture frame

Supplies
• Glazed ceramic tile, ⅜ in / 1 cm: assorted colors, 1.05 kg (700 pieces)
• Acrylic paint, sienna and white
• Grout powder

Surface
• 1 wooden picture frame, 14¼ x 16½ in / 36 x 42 cm, with a 2⅜ in / 6 cm-wide surface

How to do it
Gluing the tile
Paint the inner and outer edges of the picture frame white with the acrylic paint.
Glue the tile, varying colors and starting with the outside edge (technique on page 12).

Grout and finishing
Tint the grout with a touch of sienna paint, and follow the instructions on page 13.

Pot shard wall mosaic

Supplies
• Glazed ceramic tile, ⅜ in / 1 cm: assorted colors, 85 g (56 pieces)
• 1 small terra cotta pot, broken

Surface
• 1 linen canvas, mounted on a frame, 7⅞ x 7⅞ in / 20 x 20 cm

How to do it
Gluing the tile
Glue the tiles one at a time onto the canvas, putting a bit of glue directly onto the back of each tile (technique on page 12).
Glue the pieces of broken pot in the middle. Take care not to use too much glue, and clean off any excess glue immediately.

Grout and finishing
This mosaic doesn't use any grout.

Geometric wall mosaic

Supplies
• Glazed ceramic tile, ⅜ in / 1 cm: assorted colors, 220 g (144 pieces)
• Acrylic paint, dark brown
• Masking tape
• Grout powder

Surface
• 1 linen canvas, mounted on a frame, 7⅞ x 7⅞ in / 20 x 20 cm

How to do it
Gluing the tile
Locate the center of the canvas as best you can, and begin the gluing process with the 4 tiles surrounding that center point. Put a bit of glue directly onto the back of each tile (technique on page 12).

Grout and finishing
Put the masking tape along the cup's sides and along the edges of the mosaicked areas to keep grout off the unmosaicked canvas.
Tint the grout with the acrylic paint to make it light brown, and follow the instructions on page 13.

Flower mirror

Supplies
• Briare ceramic tile: pink, 400 g (80 pieces); fuchsia, 300 g (60 pieces)
• Ceramic pebble tiles: dark pink, 24 small tiles
• 8 glass pebbles, pink
• Acrylic paint, white
• Grout powder

Surface
• 1 mirror with a fiberboard frame in the shape of a flower

How to do it

Preparing the surface
Remove the mirror from the frame and put it safely out of the way. Paint the inner and outer edges of the frame white with the acrylic paint.

With a pencil, mark the locations of the 4 flowers and the 4 lone glass pebbles.

Cutting and gluing the tile
Cut the fuchsia tiles into 9 equal squares (technique on page 11) and glue them around the inner and outer edges of the frame's surface.
Next, put together the flowers: Start by gluing the glass pebbles, and then place the ceramic pebble tiles around them for petals.
Next, glue the lone glass pebbles. Fill in the remaining area with the pink tiles, cut into irregular shapes (technique on page 11). Cut any remaining fuchsia tiles the same way, and glue a single piece of fuchsia here and there as you go.

Grout and finishing
Follow the instructions on page 13.
Put the mirror back into place.

Polka-dot mirror

Supplies
- Briare ceramic tile: fuchsia, 100 g (20 pieces); blue, 100 g (20 pieces); yellow-green, 400 g (80 pieces)
- Acrylic paint, fuchsia
- Grout powder

Surface
- 1 mirror with a fiberboard frame in the shape of a heart

How to do it

Preparing the surface
Remove the mirror from the frame and put it safely out of the way. Paint the inner and outer edges of the frame fuchsia with the acrylic paint.
With a pencil, draw circles of various sizes on the frame.

Cutting and gluing the tile
Decide which circles will be which color, and trim the fuchsia and blue tiles to size accordingly (technique on page 11). Glue the circular tesserae in position.
Cut the yellow-green tiles into irregular shapes (technique on page 11).
Glue the resulting pieces of yellow-green to the frame, starting with the inner and outer edges of the surface and then filling in the remaining area. Try to space the tesserae evenly. Let dry.

Grout and finishing
Follow the instructions on page 13.
Put the mirror back into place.

Southwestern-style mirror

Supplies
• Briare ceramic tile: black, 50 g (10 pieces); orange, 300 g (60 pieces); brown, 100 g (20 pieces)
• Ceramic pebble tiles: sand, 2 large, 8 medium, and 160 small tiles
• Acrylic paint, pale yellow
• Grout powder

Surface
• 1 mirror with a wide, pointed fiberboard frame

How to do it

Preparing the surface
Remove the mirror from the frame and put it safely out of the way. Paint the inner and outer edges of the frame pale yellow with the acrylic paint.
With a pencil, mark out the various "color zones" (see photo for guidance).

Cutting and gluing the tile
Glue 1 large ceramic pebble tile to the central point on each side of the frame. Glue the small pebble tiles around the inner and outer edges of the frame's surface. Then, fill in the triangular areas above and below the mirror with small and medium pebble tiles. Glue a few of the remaining pebble tiles at random, in places where they'll be surrounded by square ceramic tile.
Cut the black square ceramic tile into irregular shapes (technique on page 11), and glue them in the triangular areas to either side of the mirror.
Cut the orange and brown square ceramicl tiles the same way, and use them to fill in the remaining area, doing your best to space them evenly.

Grout and finishing
Follow the instructions on page 13.
Put the mirror back into place.

Lizard

Supplies
• Briare ceramic tile: light brown, 50 g (10 pieces); dark brown, 150 g (30 pieces); yellow, 50 g (10 pieces); green, 10 g (2 pieces); black, 10 g (2 pieces)
• Grout powder

Surface
• 1 surface in the shape of a lizard

How to do it

Cutting and gluing the tile
Start with the lizard's tail. Cut 1 dark brown tile into a triangle for the tip of the tail, and then cut additional dark brown tiles into rectangles of various sizes. Glue these rectangles along the edges of the tail, with small rectangles near the tip and progressively larger rectangles toward the base. Cut some of the yellow tiles into narrow trapezoids, to fit the space that opens up between the dark brown rectangles as you near the base of the tail, and glue them into place. Cut some more dark brown tiles into small squares (technique on page 11) and glue them around the outer edge of the rest of the lizard's body. Using the black tile, form the lizard's claws by cutting out small triangles, and the lizard's eyes by cutting 2 small ovals. For the lizard's back, cut yellow, green, and light brown tiles into diamond shapes and glue them (see photo for guidance), spacing the tesserae as evenly as possible. Fill in the remaining area with dark brown and yellow tesserae, cut into irregular shapes (technique on page 11).

Grout and finishing
Follow the instructions on page 13.

Tray

Supplies
• Square ceramic tiles, 7⅞ x 7⅞ in / 20 x 20 cm: 3 ochre, 1 yellow
• Acrylic paint, black
• Grout powder

Surface
• 1 wooden tray, 12⅜ x 19¾ in / 31.5 x 50 cm

How to do it

Cutting and gluing the tile
Cut the tiles into multiple rectangles of varying sizes (technique on page 14), and arrange them in a pattern on the tray's surface. Once you're satisfied with your design, glue the pieces into place. Let dry.

Grout and finishing
Tint the grout with the acrylic paint to make it gray, and then follow the instructions on page 13.

Frame

Supplies
• Square ceramic tiles, 7⅞ x 7⅞ in / 20 x 20 cm: 2 ochre, 1 yellow
• Acrylic paint, black
• Grout powder

Surface
• 1 wooden picture frame, 10⅝ x 13 in / 27 x 33 cm, with a 2 in / 5 cm-wide frame

How to do it

Cutting and gluing the tile
Cut enough small squares of tile to cover the inside and outside edges of the frame (technique on page 11). Cut multiple rectangles of varying sizes (technique on page 14), and arrange them in a pattern on the frame's surface. Once you're satisfied with your design, glue the pieces into place. Start with the small squares on the inside and outside edges, and let dry before gluing the main motif. Let dry again before applying grout.

Grout and finishing
Tint the grout with the acrylic paint to make it gray, and then follow the instructions on page 13.

Pots, small bowls, and accessories

* * * * * * * * * * * * * * * * * * *

materials

❖ Tile nippers
❖ Craft tweezers
❖ Potters' rib
❖ Spoon
❖ Brush
❖ Pencil
❖ Marker
❖ Small jar
❖ Dry cloth
❖ White vinegar

Assorted pots

* * * * * * * * * * * * * * * * * *

Supplies **(for 2 pots)**
• Briare ceramic tile: pale pink, 200 g (40 pieces); bright pink, 320 g (64 pieces); dark pink, 200 g (40 pieces)
• Acrylic paint, black
• Grout powder

Surface
• 2 terra cotta pots, 6 in / 15 cm diameter

How to do it

Preparing the surface
Begin by copying the drawing of the salamander (see page 60), either freehand or by using carbon paper.

Cutting and gluing the tile
Divide each of the tiles into about 3 pieces, cutting them into irregular shapes (technique on page 11). Don't hesitate to make some of the pieces very small. Glue the tesserae to the pots, starting with the salamanders (technique on page 12) and then filling in the remaining area.
Let dry.

Grout and finishing
Tint the grout with the acrylic paint to make it gray, and then follow the instructions on page 13.

Key tray

* * * * * * * * * * * * * * * * *

Supplies
• Briare ceramic tile: pale pink, 225 g (45 pieces); bright pink, 100 g (20 pieces); dark pink, 150 g (30 pieces)
• Acrylic paint, black
• Grout powder

Surface
• 1 wooden key tray, 8⅝ in x 8⅝ in / 22 x 22 cm

How to do it

Preparing the surface
If your key tray is unfinished wood, you can leave it that way—or you can paint it before starting your mosaic. Begin by copying the drawing of the salamander (see page 60), either freehand or by using carbon paper.

Cutting and gluing the tile
Cut some pale pink tiles into irregular shapes (technique on page 11) and glue them down so that they fill the salamander.
Glue bright pink and pale pink tile around the edges, alternating a row of pale pink with a row of bright pink. Cut the dark pink tiles into irregular shapes (technique on page 11) and fill in the remaining area around the salamander.

Grout and finishing
Tint the grout with the acrylic paint to make it gray, and then follow the instructions on page 13.

Outdoor
mosaic

Salamander drawing
(actual size)

Planter

✳✳✳✳✳✳✳✳✳✳✳✳✳✳

Supplies

• Briare ceramic tile: red, 300 g (60 pieces); light green, 250 g (50 pieces); light yellow, 100 g (20 pieces); orange, 50 g (10 pieces)
• 10 glass pebbles, red
• Masking tape
• Acrylic paint, black and white
• Grout powder

Surface

• 1 square terra cotta planter, 9⅝ x 9⅝ in / 24.5 x 24.5 cm around and 9½ in / 24 cm deep

How to do it

Cutting and gluing the tile

With a pencil, draw 2 parallel lines, 4⅜ in / 11 cm apart, so that they form a stripe around the middle of the planter. Cut the red tiles into 2 equal rectangles, and glue them along the upper line, alternating between vertical and horizontal alignment.
Cut the light green tiles in half the same way, and glue them below the red rectangles so that red and light green together form a square.

Cut some of the yellow tiles into 4 equal squares, and glue them in the middle of the squares formed by the red and light green rectangles.
Repeat along the lower line (see photo for guidance). Finish the mosaic by filling in the remaining area in the middle with red, light yellow, and orange rectangles, placing 2 glass pebbles on each of 2 sides of the planter, and 3 glass pebbles on the other 2 sides.

Grout and finishing

Put the masking tape along the edges of the mosaicked areas to keep grout off the unmosaicked terra cotta.
Tint the grout with the black acrylic paint to make it dark gray, and then follow the instructions on page 13. Paint the top edges of the planter white.

Colorful pot

Supplies
• Briare ceramic tile: yellow, 200 g (40 pieces); red, 200 g (40 pieces); orange, 200 g (40 pieces)
• 5 opaque glass pebbles, orange
• Grout powder

Surface
• 1 pot cover, 4¾ in / 12 cm diameter and 4¾ in / 12 cm deep

How to do it

Cutting and gluing the tile
Start at the base of the pot cover. Cut some of the red tiles into 2 equal rectangles and glue them horizontally (technique on page 12).
Divide some yellow and orange tiles into triangles, cutting them in 2 diagonally and then in 2 again. Arrange them as shown in the photo. Glue the glass pebbles down, spacing them evenly around the pot cover. Cut some yellow and orange tiles into narrow rectangles (1 narrow rectangle = ⅓ of a tile), and glue these into the spaces between the glass pebbles. Glue another paired row of yellow and orange triangles, and then another row of red rectangles, oriented horizontally. Finish with a row of narrow rectangles, oriented vertically, mixing any remaining colors as desired. Let dry.

Grout and finishing
Follow the instructions on page 13.

Tart tealights

✳✱✳✱✳✱✳✱✳✱✳✱✳✱✳✱✳✱✳✱✳✱✳✱✳✱✳✱✳✱✳✱✳

Supplies **(for 3 tealights)**
• Transparent glass tile, ¾ in / 2 cm: shades of pink, 300 g (100 pieces); shades of blue, 300 g (100 pieces); shades of green, 300 g (100 pieces)
• Millefiori glass tiles: 8 yellow and blue (pink tealight); 8 orange and blue (blue tealight); 8 red and white (green tealight)
• Glass mosaic glue

Surface
3 glasses, 3 in / 7.5 cm diameter and 3⅜ in / 8.5 cm deep

How to do it
Cutting and gluing the tile
Note: Glass mosaic glue requires careful handling. Do not get any glue on the outer faces of the tiles; it will be very difficult to remove. Be precise, and don't hesitate to wipe your hands regularly to ensure that you don't smear glue around by accident. Hold the glass horizontally while you glue tiles to the side that faces upward; otherwise, the tiles may slide around in the wet glue.

Cut the tiles into rectangles and squares (technique on page 11). Glue them to the glasses, one set of colors for each glass; fit them together as neatly as possible, varying shades to avoid forming distinct lines or sections. Place a millefiori tile every now and then. To emphasize the interplay of shapes and sizes, place a few tiles without cutting them at all—but not more than 3 per glass.

Grout and finishing
These mosaics don't use any grout.
Let dry thoroughly before use.

Small bowls

✳✳✳✳✳✳✳✳✳✳✳✳✳

Supplies **(for each small bowl)**
• Stone tile, ¾ in / 2 cm: light green, 90 g (30 pieces); dark green, 90 g (30 pieces)
• Grout powder, gray

Surface
• 2 terra cotta plant saucers, 7⅞ in / 20 cm diameter

How to do it

Cutting and gluing the tile

Start by cutting 9 dark green tiles into quarters, and glue those pieces around the outside edge of the first saucer (technique on page 12). Next, cut 16 dark green tiles into 2, and glue the resulting rectangles around the inside lip, oriented vertically. You may have to bevel the corners of some of the rectangles slightly for fit (technique on page 11).

Cut 11 light green tiles into 2, and glue the resulting rectangles around the remaining edge surface, oriented horizontally. They should cover the edges of the first two sets of tesserae. Pay attention to the amount of space available; try to space the tesserae evenly. You may have to trim a couple of rectangles to help with fit, but you don't want any of the tesserae to be dramatically narrower than their neighbors.

Cut the rest of the tiles into irregular shapes (technique on page 11).

Copy the image of the cactus onto the interior surface of the saucer, either freehand or with carbon paper. Glue the rest of the tesserae, filling in the cactus first and then the remaining area. Again, try to space the tesserae as evenly as possible.

Let dry.

Repeat with the second plant saucer, reversing the colors.

Grout and finishing

Add a little extra powder to the grout to make it thicker, and follow the instructions on page 13.

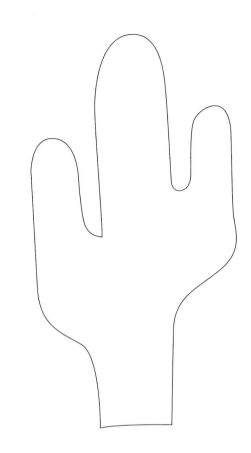

Cactus drawing (actual size)

Seize-the-day tray

✳✳✳✳✳✳✳✳✳✳✳✳✳✳✳

Supplies
- Briare ceramic tile: yellow, 300 g (60 pieces); red, 200 g (40 pieces)
- Acrylic paint, yellow and red
- Stencils or stamps of your choice
- Grout powder
- Varnish

Surface
- 1 tray, 11 x 11 in / 28 x 28 cm, 3⅛ in / 8 cm deep

How to do it

Preparing the surface
Freehand or using carbon paper, copy the flower design below onto the interior bottom surface of the tray. Paint the tray yellow with the acrylic paint, except for the interior bottom surface.

Cutting the tile
When cutting, don't worry about making the shapes absolutely perfect. Grout tends to disguise any minor mistakes you might make.

- **The center of the flower**

Cut 1 red tile into quarters (technique on page 12), and, using a marker, draw a circle on the back of one of the squares. With tile nippers, cut and trim the tile until you've obtained the shape desired.

- **The petals**

Cut red tiles into irregular shapes (technique on page 11) of the approximate dimensions necessary. Round 2 corners on 10 of these pieces to shape the ends of the petals.

- **The background**

Cut the yellow tiles into irregular shapes (technique on page 11).

Gluing the tile
Start by gluing the center of the flower into place, and then glue the petals around it. Don't hesitate to trim a tessera if you find yourself wanting to refine the shape. Fill in the remaining area around the flower with the yellow tesserae. Let dry.

Grout and finishing
Follow the instructions on page 13. If any grout ends up on the sides of the tray during the application process, clean it off as quickly as possible. Use stencils or stamps for the writing and the flower on the outside of the tray. Varnishing the tray, mosaicked portion included, will make it easy to clean.

Flower design (actual size)

Birdhouse

✳✳✳✳✳✳✳✳✳✳✳

Supplies
• Briare ceramic tile: sand, 150 g (30 pieces); yellow, 10 g (2 pieces); red, 10 g (2 pieces); light blue, 30 g (6 pieces); dark blue, 30 g (6 pieces); light green, 20 g (4 pieces); dark green, 20 g (4 pieces)
• Grout powder
• Semi-glossy varnish

Surface
• 1 wooden birdhouse

How to do it

Cutting and gluing the tile
Note: Cutting tile to a curve requires patience, time, and a helping hand. You may want to have some extra tiles on hand.

Roof: Divide the sand tiles into quarters (technique on page 11). Glue them onto both sides of the roof.
Butterfly: On the faces (not the backs) of the red tiles, use a marker to draw the shapes of the wings (2 large, 2 small). Trim the tiles into the desired shape a bit at a time; don't worry about making the shape absolutely perfect. Grout tends to disguise any minor mistakes you might make. Glue the butterfly together just below the entrance to the birdhouse.
Sun: Draw a half-circle on 1 of the yellow tiles and cut, just as you did for the curves of the butterfly's wings. Glue the sun just under the edge of one side of the roof. On the other yellow tile, draw and then cut out the rays of the sun, little by little. Glue them around the sun in a semicircle.
Grass: Cut the light green and dark green tiles into irregular shapes (technique on page 11). Glue them over the lower third of the front of the birdhouse. Try to keep the spacing between tesserae as even as possible.
Sky: Cut the light blue and dark blue tiles into irregular shapes (technique on page 11). Fill in the remaining area on the front of the birdhouse.
Let dry.

Grout and finishing
Follow the instructions on page 13.
Varnish the parts of the birdhouse not covered by mosaic.

Letter coasters

Supplies (for 6 coasters)
- Micro-mosaic tiles, ⅜ in / 1 cm: pink, 40 g; yellow, 40 g; green, 30 g
- Micro-mosaic tiles, ³⁄₁₆ in / 5 mm: pink, 40 g; yellow, 40 g; green, 40 g
- Acrylic paint, green, yellow, and pink
- Grout powder

Surface
- 6 wooden coasters with wavy edges

How to do it

Preparing the surface
Draw the letters you want to mosaic onto the coasters. Paint the edges and the backs of the coasters with the acrylic paint: two with green, two with pink, and two with yellow.

Cutting and gluing the tile
Glue the ⅜ in / 1 cm micro-mosaic tiles onto the letters, matching the color of each letter to the color you painted the coaster. For letters with curves bevel some of the tiles into trapezoids to fit (technique on page 11). Next, glue ³⁄₁₆ in / 5 mm tiles around the edges of the coasters, in the same colors as the letters, beveling as necessary to fit curves (technique on page 11).
Fill in the remaining area with ³⁄₁₆ in / 5 mm tiles, varying colors so that each coaster uses two colors of tile and no two coasters are exactly the same. Try not to lay the tiles in straight lines, but keep the spacing between them as even as possible.

Grout and finishing
Follow the instructions on page 13.

Doorplate

****

Supplies (for the "7" mosaic shown)
• Briare ceramic tile: light blue, 100 g (20 pieces); white, 150 g (30 pieces); fuchsia, 5 g (1 piece)
• Ceramic pebble tiles: dark blue, 4 medium and 11 small tiles
• Acrylic paint, light gray
• Grout powder

Surface
• 1 fiberboard plaque, 8¼ x 11¾ in / 21 x 30 cm, at least 3/16 in / 5 mm thick, with wavy edges

How to do it

Preparing the surface
If you need to make a doorplate with multiple digits, orient the plaque horizontally. With a pencil, draw the desired number in the middle of the surface.

Cutting and gluing the tile
Glue the ceramic pebble tiles in position to form the numbers.
With 3 of the remaining pebble tiles, glue a flower in the lower right corner of the plaque.
Cut the light blue and fuchsia tiles into 2, and then cut each half into 4 small narrow rectangles (technique on page 11).

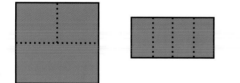

Glue the light blue rectangles around the edges of the plaque. Near the top left corner, insert the fuchsia rectangles amidst the light blue. Cut the white tiles into irregular shapes (technique on page 11) and fill in the remaining area, doing your best to space the pieces evenly. Let dry.

Grout and finishing
Tint the grout with the acrylic paint to make it light gray, and follow the instructions on page 13.
Paint the edges of the plaque with the acrylic paint.

Starfish

****

Supplies
• Iridescent glass tile, ¾ in / 2 cm: white, 150 g (50 pieces); light blue, 200 g (67 pieces); dark blue, 50 g (17 pieces)
• 3 glass pebbles, ultramarine
• Acrylic paint, dark blue
• Grout powder

Surface
• 1 wooden star, unfinished (or 1 piece of fiberboard, 11¾ x 11¾ in / 30 x 30 cm, at least ³/₁₆ in / 5 mm thick, cut into the shape of a star)

How to do it

Cutting and gluing the tile
It may be helpful to draw the interior star on the surface before you begin. Cut the white tiles into irregular shapes (technique on page 11) and glue them into place for the star.
Glue the 3 glass pebbles somewhere in the remaining area.
Cut the blue tiles of both shades into irregular shapes and glue them down, starting around the edges of the interior star and filling in the remaining area. Make sure you place some dark blue tesserae from time to time so you don't run out too quickly or end up with a solid dark blue area at the end.
Let dry.

Grout and finishing
Tint the grout blue with the acrylic paint and follow the instructions on page 13.
Paint the edges of the star with the acrylic paint.

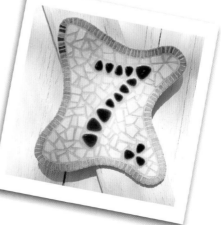

Welcoming sun

✳✳✳✳✳✳✳✳✳✳✳✳✳✳✳

Supplies
- Briare ceramic tile: brown, 200 g (40 pieces); beige, 200 g (40 pieces); yellow, 50 g (10 pieces)
- Acrylic paint, brown
- Grout powder

Surface
- 1 piece of fiberboard, 7⅞ x 9⅞ in / 20 x 25 cm, at least ³⁄₁₆ in / 5 mm thick, with wavy edges

How to do it

Preparing the surface
Paint the edges of the fiberboard brown with the acrylic paint.

With a pencil, draw the number or numbers desired in the middle of the surface. Draw a sun in one corner, making sure to leave enough space for the border.

Cutting and gluing the tile
Cut the brown tiles into 3 rectangles, and then cut each rectangle into 3 small squares. For numbers with straight lines (like the 1 in the photo), use larger tesserae—trim the rectangles to fit instead of cutting them into squares. Round the outer edges of the tesserae at the ends. For curvy numbers (like the 6 in the photo), bevel the squares into trapezoids for fit (technique on page 11). Glue the brown tesserae in place to form the numbers.

For the middle of the sun, draw a circle with a marker on the back of one of the small brown squares. Trim the square down to the line with tile nippers—don't worry about trying to make it absolutely perfect. For the rays of the sun, draw 10 irregular, tapering waves onto brown tiles and then trim them out. Glue the sun and its rays in place.

For the border, cut more brown tiles into small squares, again beveling the corners for fit as necessary (technique on page 11). Glue the squares into place around the edge.

Cut beige, yellow, and brown tiles into irregular shapes (technique on page 11) and fill in the remaining area—mostly with beige, placing yellow and brown pieces from time to time.

Grout and finishing
Follow the instructions on page 13.

Outdoor furniture

Pedestal table

materials

✤ Tile nippers
✤ Craft tweezers
✤ Potters' rib
✤ Spoon
✤ Brush
✤ Pencil
✤ Marker
✤ Small jar
✤ Dry cloth
✤ White vinegar

Supplies
• Briare ceramic tile: dark blue, 400 g (80 pieces); sea-blue, 150 g (30 pieces); white, 400 g (80 pieces)
• Acrylic paint, white and turquoise
• Grout powder

Surface
• 1 fiberboard pedestal table, 9 x 14½ in / 23 x 37 cm, and 15¾ in / 40 cm tall

How to do it

Preparing the surface
Start by painting the edges of the flat surfaces and the legs of the table white, and the outer edges of the legs turquoise. Let dry. (It's also entirely possible to paint remaining surfaces after completing the mosaic, but you'll have to be careful not to get paint on the mosaic tiles.)

Cutting and gluing the tile
With a pencil, draw two lines that cross in the center of both the upper and lower surfaces.
For the upper surface, glue the 3 center tiles as shown in the diagram, 2 sea-blue and 1 dark blue, making sure they are square with your lines (technique on page 78) and centered on top of them.

Continue gluing along the horizontal line you drew, centering each tile over the line and alternating colors until you've glued 4 tiles on either side of the center tile. Complete the checkerboard rectangle (see photo for guidance). Make sure all the tiles are square with your lines and with each other, and evenly spaced.
Cut some dark blue tiles in 2 diagonally to create triangles, and glue the triangles around the edges of the checkerboard. Cut 4 more dark blue tiles into rectangles ⅝ in / 1.5 cm wide, and glue them at the corners of the upper surface, lining them up with the legs of the table.
Cut additional dark blue tiles into quarters (technique on page 11) and glue them around the edge of the upper surface.
Complete the mosaic by cutting white tile and a few sea-blue tiles into irregular shapes (technique on page 11) and filling in the remaining area with them, spacing them as evenly as possible.
Repeat with the lower surface of the table. For a checkerboard pattern only 2 tiles across, glue 4 central tiles so that their corners meet where your pencil lines cross.

Grout and finishing
Follow the instructions on page 13.

Garden table

Supplies

- Stone tile, ¾ in / 2 cm: white, 660 g (220 pieces); brown, 660 g (220 pieces); pale green, 390 g (130 pieces); arctic blue, 240 g (80 pieces)
- Wire brush
- Anti-rust paint, black
- Grout powder, black
- Flat plastic trim/edging/molding, black
- White pencil
- Liquid soap
- Varnish

Surface

- 1 round iron table, 23⅝ in / 60 cm diameter

Before

How to do it

Preparing the surface

Scrub the surface with the wire brush to remove any rust. Cover the bare iron with 2 coats of the anti-rust paint. Let dry. With the pencil, draw two straight lines so that they cross at right angles in the center of the table.

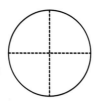

Cutting and gluing the tile

Start by gluing 1 white tile in the center (technique on page 12), right where the lines cross, making sure it is square to both lines.
Then glue additional white tile in rows, moving outward along each line to the edge and spacing the tiles as evenly as possible. Center the tiles over the lines and make sure they are square to the lines and each other.

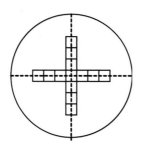

Glue squares of 9 arctic blue tiles apiece in each corner formed by the central X. Continue laying out the rest of the pattern (see photo for guidance), always making sure each tile is as square to the others as possible. Trim the tiles along the edge with tile nippers to fit (technique on page 11).
Let dry thoroughly.

Grout and finishing

With a carbide hand file, smooth the edges of the table. Dark-colored or black grout, when freshly mixed and wet, can stain tiles; to avoid this, cover the mosaic with a thin coating of soap. You'll need to try to avoid scraping the tiles while you are applying grout, so as not to rub off the soap.
Follow the instructions on page 13. After 30 minutes of drying time, clean with a sponge, rinsing the sponge frequently. There should still be some excess grout left on the mosaic.
Let dry 48 hours and clean with white vinegar.
Apply a coat of varnish to the mosaic to protect it. Use the plastic edging/molding to cover the edges of the mosaic.

After

Suppliers

D&L Art Glass Supply
www.dlstainedglass.com
Phone: 800-525-0940
info@dlartglass.com

Delphi Glass
www.delphiglass.com
Phone: 800-248-2048

Ed Hoy's Int'l
www.edhoy.com
Phone: 800-323-5668
info@edhoy.com

Glass Crafter's Stained Glass Supply
www.glasscrafters.com
Phone: 800-422-4552
info@glasscrafters.biz

Maryland Mosaics
www.marylandmosaics.com
Phone: 410-356-3555
info@marylandmosaics.com

Mosaic Mercantile
www.mosaicmercantile.com
Phone: 877-966-7242
info@mosaicmercantile.com

MosaicSmalti
www.mosaicsmalti.com
Phone: 508-432-5369

WitsEnd Mosaics
www.witsendmosaic.com
Phone: 888-494-8736

ORIGAMI MAGIC

No part of this publication may be reproduced in whole or in part, or stored in a retrieval system, or transmitted in any form or by any means, electronic, mechanical, photocopying, recording, or otherwise, without written permission of the publisher. For information regarding permission, write to Scholastic Inc., 730 Broadway, New York, NY 10003.

ISBN 0-590-47124-4

12 11 10 9 8 7 6 5 4 3 2 1   3 4 5 6 7 8/9

Printed in the U.S.A.   08

First Scholastic printing, November 1993

FLORENCE TEMKO
ORIGAMI MAGIC

Drawings by Sandra Denis and Florence Temko
Photographs by Dan Wagner
Designed by Hollie A. Rubin

SCHOLASTIC INC.
New York Toronto London Auckland Sydney

CONTENTS

INTRODUCTION

Origami is magic because you can make all kinds of neat things just by folding a piece of paper. If you've ever flown a paper airplane, you have already done origami. With the help of this book you can send a secret valentine, hang up shiny Christmas stars, display a proud peacock, set a Thanksgiving turkey on the dinner table, surprise your cousins with a magic circle, produce beautiful birthday cards in a few minutes, or make earrings for a friend. Give them away, display them, collect them. Amaze your friends and make new ones.

Origami is a Japanese word that means "paper folding" (*ori* = folding, *gami* = paper). The word is adopted from Japan, where origami is a traditional craft, but paperfolding is now a popular hobby with people in many countries. It's multicultural, inexpensive, and recyclable.

Paperfolders like to teach each other origami or learn new models from books. Some invent their own designs, which are then identified with their names in much the same way as the names of painters and sculptors are associated with their works of art.

For more information about paperfolders or groups that meet in your area, or anything else about origami, contact:

Friends of the Origami Center, 620
15 West 77th Street
New York, NY 10024

To receive a reply to your request, you must enclose a self-addressed envelope with *double* letter postage.

Let's go with origami!

Most given measurements are suggestions. You can use smaller or larger pieces of paper.

PAPERS TO USE

You can buy paper squares made specially for origami. They are colored on one side and white on the other, and designed to hold sharp creases. They are sold in packets in many art and museum stores, Asian and gift shops.

At home and in school you can find other kinds of fairly thin papers that are very suitable and cheaper. Recycle used stationery, computer sheets, gift wrap, foil gift wrap, shopping bags, and magazine pages. Cut them into squares with scissors or, more easily, on a paper cutter.

LAMINATING PAPERS FOR LONG LIFE

If you want to preserve your completed origamis, cover them with one or more layers of white glue (which dries clear) or clear acrylic spray. For a really hard finish, use a brush-on or dipping glaze.

YOU MUST WATCH FOR THESE SIGNS

When You See This:		It Means:
Broken Line	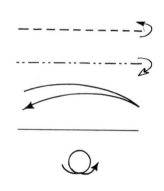	Valley Fold (fold up)
Line of Dashes and Dots		Mountain Fold (fold back)
Double Arrow		Fold/Unfold
Thin Line		A Crease You Made Before
Rolled Arrow		Turn Paper Over

HOW TO CUT A SQUARE FROM A RECTANGLE OF PAPER

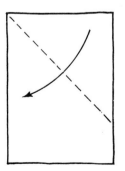

1. Fold the short edge of the paper to the long edge, through the middle of the corner.

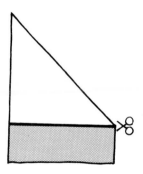

2. Cut off the area shown shaded.

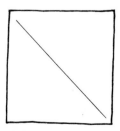

3. Unfold and here is your square.

IDEAS FOR USING ORIGAMI

You can share origami in many practical ways, and here are a few suggestions. Invent other applications yourself.

FOR GREETING CARDS

Secret Friend's Knot, Ladybug, Fish, My Pet Puppy, Ice Cream Cone, Tree, Santa Claus or Troll, Turkey, Dinosaur, Heart Valentine, Party Hat, Sailboat, Flapping Bird.

FOR HOLIDAY ORNAMENTS, TO HANG OR SET ON A TABLE

Magic Fortune Teller, Ladybug, Fish, Butterfly, Santa Claus, Turkey, Proud Peacock, Star, Ball, Magic Circle, Airplane, International Peace Crane. (Almost all origamis can be used as hanging ornaments, especially when made from shiny foil gift wrap.)

FOR PARTY DECORATIONS AND FAVORS

Magic Fortune Teller Party Dish and Cat Puppet, My Pet Puppy, Fans, Santa Claus or Troll, Masks, Turkey, Proud Peacock, Dinosaur, Heart Valentine, Party Hat, Star, Flower, Magic Circle, UFO Flower, Friendly Frog, Magic Hopping Bunny, Junk Box, Basket, Airplane, Square Base Puppet, Helicopter, International Peace Crane, Flapping Bird.

FOR GROUP AND PARTY FUN

Fishing Game, Masks, Turkey, Friendly Frog Party Game, Airplane (as a competition), Square Base Puppet, International Peace Crane.

FOR EARRINGS AND PINS

You can turn many origamis into jewelry when you begin with small paper squares. Try the Magic Fortune Teller, Fan Earrings, Heart Pin, Combination Triangle and Square Bases. For earrings, attach loops of thread to fit around your ears. Or you can buy wire loops and clips suitable for pierced and unpierced ears. They are sold in craft and bead stores.

FOR GIFTS

Any origami.

FOR STORYTELLING

Any animal or puppet.

*MAGIC FORTUNE TELLER

The Magic Fortune Teller is a very popular paperfold, but most people don't know that it can be turned into many other things. Find out how to fold the basic Magic Fortune Teller and then turn it into a Cat Puppet or a Party Dish.

YOU NEED

A square of paper, about 6″ (15 cm)

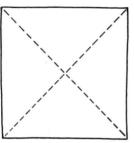

1. Fold the square on both diagonals. Unfold paper flat each time.

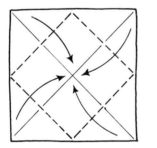

2. Fold all four corners to meet in the center.

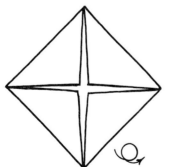

3. *Flip the paper over from front to back.*

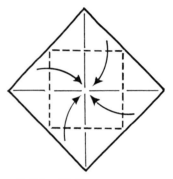

4. Again, fold all four corners to the center.

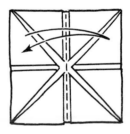

5. Fold paper in half from side to side. Unfold.

6. Fold paper in half from bottom to top. Do not unfold.

7. Slide both thumbs under the two little squares on the front. Slide your forefingers under the squares on the back.

8. Magic Fortune Teller.

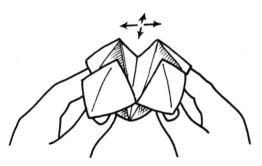

9. Move the Magic Fortune Teller like this: Push your hands close together; then push your thumbs and forefingers apart.

HOW TO TELL FORTUNES

Place the Magic Fortune Teller to look like drawing 5. Lift up the four triangles one after the other and write in a fortune. Here are some ideas, but it's even more fun to make up your own wording:

    You'll find a new friend.
    You are a monster.
    You forgot your homework.
    You'll fly to the moon.

PARTY DISH

Turn the Magic Fortune Teller upside down and fill it with nuts, raisins, and candy. Use large squares of construction paper or gift wrap doubled for extra strength.

CAT PUPPET

Draw eyes and whiskers on the Magic Fortune Teller. Move it up and down while you say "meow," or make up a story about a family of cats.

*SECRET FRIEND'S KNOT

The Secret Friend's Knot is a good way to send a private message to a friend. At one time valentines were folded in this way.

YOU NEED

A sheet of notepaper or stationery

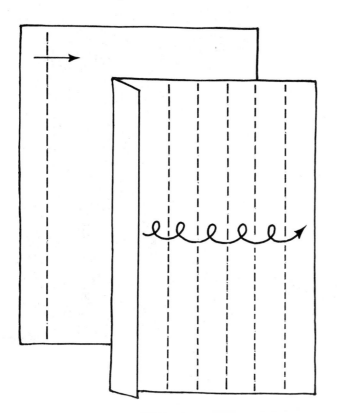

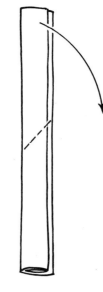

3. At about the middle, fold the strip at a right angle to the right.

1. Fold the long edge over about 1″ (3 cm).

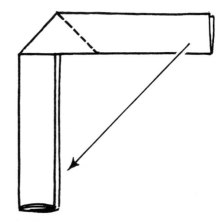

2. Keep folding the paper over and over into a narrow strip.

4. Fold the strip down.

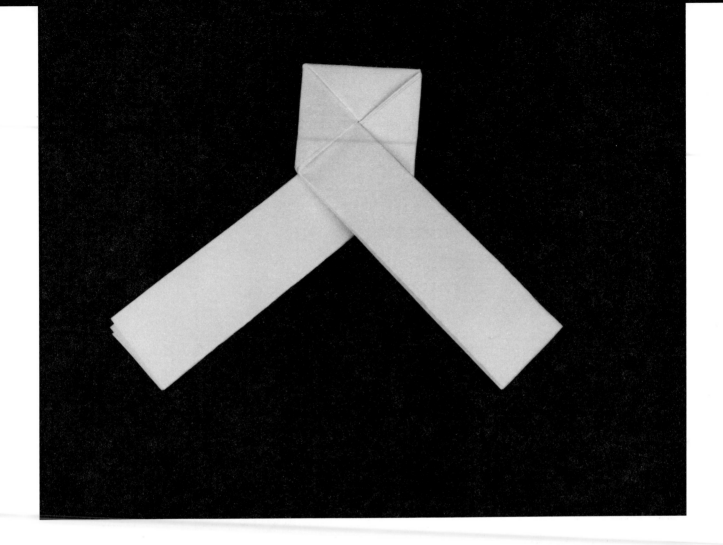

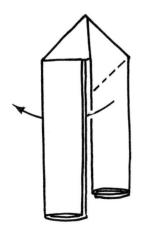

5. Fold the strip to the left and tuck it under.

6. Secret Friend's Knot.

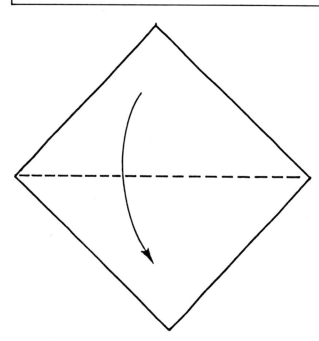

1. Fold corner to corner.

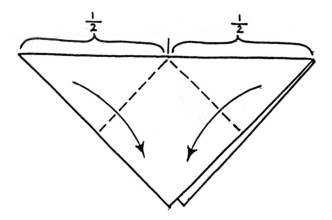

2. Fold the outside corners down, but leave a gap in between. See next drawing.

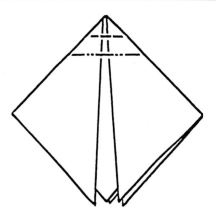

3. Form the head by folding the top down and then back again, in a pleat.

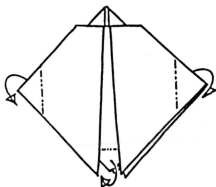

4. Round the body by folding back the two outside corners and the corner under the wings. (You'll have small triangles at the sides and the tail on the underside of the bug. If you like, you can tuck them in between the main layers of paper. This gives a neater look preferred by paperfolders. It's called reverse folding.)

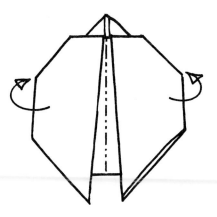

WIGGLY BUG

Place the Ladybug on your hand. When you move your hand the Ladybug wiggles. Make up a story about your Wiggly Bug and tell it to a friend.

5. Make the Ladybug three-dimensional. Fold the body in half. Then open the paper again until it is not quite flat.

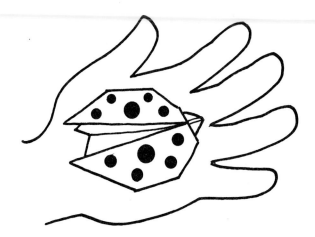

6. Ladybug.

*FISH

YOU NEED

A square of paper, about 5″ (13 cm)
If paper is colored on one side only, begin with white side up.

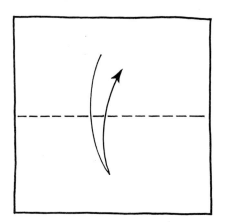

1. Fold paper in half. Unfold.

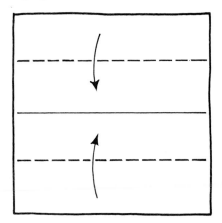

2. Fold edges to the crease.

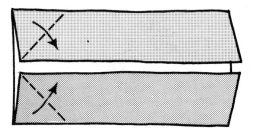

3. Fold two corners to the middle.

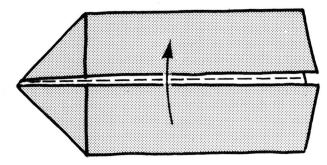

4. Fold paper in half.

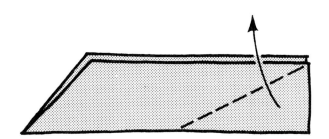

5. Twist up the bottom corner.

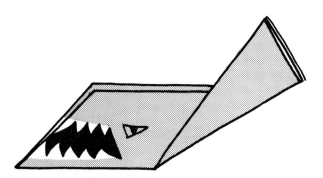

6. Fish.

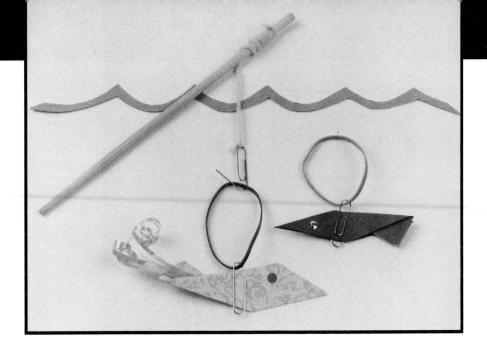

FISHING GAME

YOU NEED
Squares of paper, about 3"
(8 cm), each in different colors
Rubber bands
Paper clips
String or yarn
A pencil or chopstick or dowel

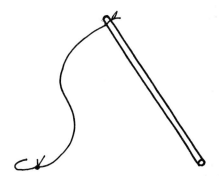

2. Make a fishing rod. Tie a piece of string or yarn around one end of a pencil, chopstick, or dowel. Bend open one end of a paper clip and knot it to the other end of the string.

HOW TO PLAY THE GAME

Put out a lot of Fish. Each color Fish has a different value. Let's say blue Fish are worth 5 points, yellow Fish are worth 10 points, and red Fish are worth 20 points. Each player takes a turn at catching a Fish. When all the Fish have been caught, the player with the most points wins.

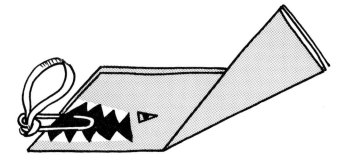

1. Make a lot of Fish. For each Fish, twist and double a rubber band; attach it to a paper clip. Slide the paper clip onto a Fish.

YOU NEED

Two squares of construction paper, about 6″ (15 cm) each

HEAD *Use one square.*

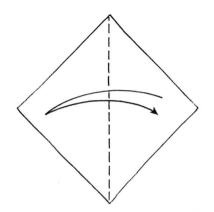

1. Fold corner to corner. Unfold paper flat.

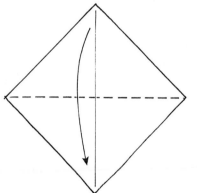

2. Fold top corner to bottom corner.

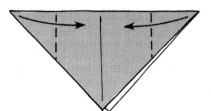

3. Fold both outside corners to the crease.

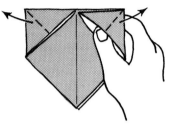

4. Push your finger inside one triangle and spread it apart. Press it flat into a square. Repeat on the other side.

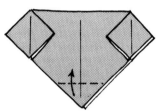

5. Fold up the bottom corner, one layer of paper only.

6. Head.

BODY *Use the other square.*

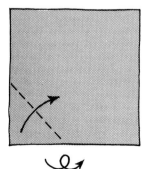

1. Fold up tip of one corner. Turn paper over to the other side.

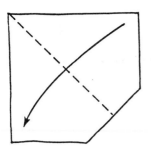

2. Fold corner to corner.

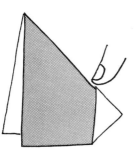

3. Pull the corner away and crease the tail to stay in place.

4. Body.

ASSEMBLY

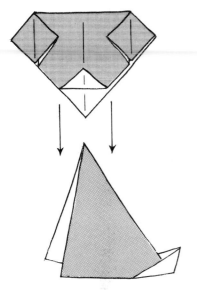

1. Place head on top of the body.

2. My Pet Puppy.

TABLE DECORATIONS

Make a Puppy for each person to take home. Or give paper squares to your guests and teach them to make their own party favors.

PUPPY PUPPET

Fold the head. Hold it with two hands, as shown. To move the puppet, push hands to each other and apart. Make barking noises. Use puppets as characters to tell a story.

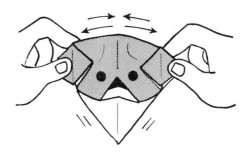

*FANS

On a hot day it's nice to cool yourself with a fan. You probably already know how to fold one, but here is a way that helps you crease neat, straight pleats. Any rectangle will do, but three times as long as wide is a good proportion.

YOU NEED

A rectangle of paper, about 5″ by 15″ (13 cm by 38 cm)

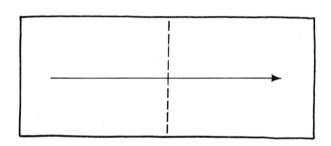

1. Fold paper in half the short way.

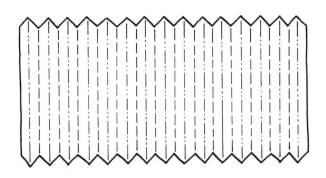

3. Open paper flat. Pleat the paper up and down on the creased lines (mountain and valley folds). Fold over one end of the fan (or staple it). Spread the other end.

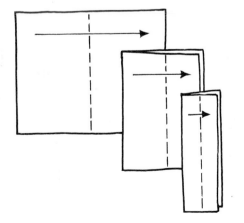

2. Fold it in half three more times.

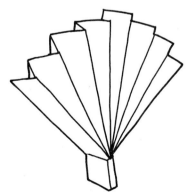

4. Fan.

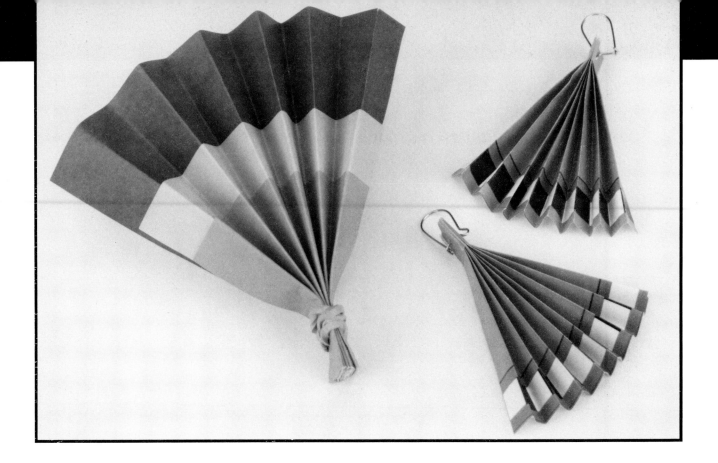

EARRINGS

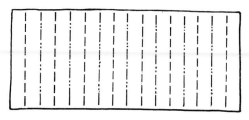

1. Pleat fans from paper 2″ by 5″ (5 cm by 3 cm).

2. Wind a narrow piece of sticky tape over one end.

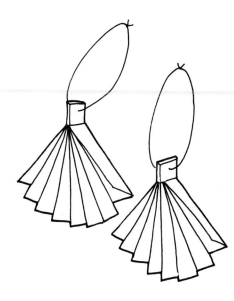

3. Spread the other end.

4. Attach earring fittings. See color photo.

You can make a beautiful Bow when you fan pleat a paper square on the diagonal. It's a simple decoration you can pin in your hair, tape on a gift package, or use as a holiday table decoration.

YOU NEED

A square of origami or gift wrap paper, about 6″ (15 cm)
Stapler or ribbon

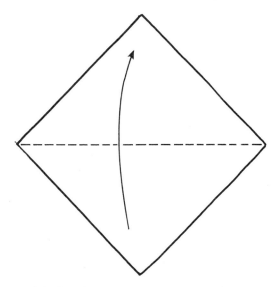

1. Fold the bottom corner to the top corner.

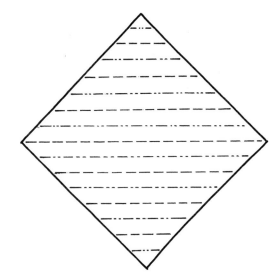

3. Pleat the paper up and down on the creased lines. Tighten the middle of the fan with a staple or ribbon.

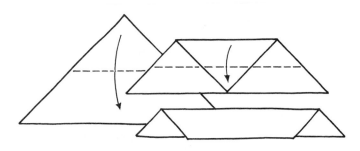

2. Fold the top of the triangle to the middle of the bottom edge. Fold from top to bottom two more times. Unfold the paper flat.

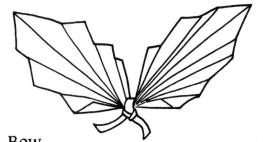

4. Bow.

BUTTERFLY

When you combine two Bows you'll have a Butterfly. Use two paper squares, one with 6″ (15 cm) sides and one with 4″ (10 cm) sides. Fasten them together with a twist tie, and let the ends stick out as feelers.

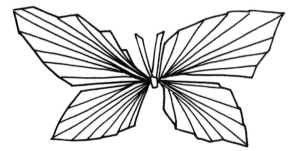

A kite shape appears when you make only three creases. This is called the Kite Base, which is the beginning of many other origamis. Some of them are shown on the next few pages.

YOU NEED

A square of paper, about 6″ (15 cm)
If paper is colored on one side only, begin with white side up.

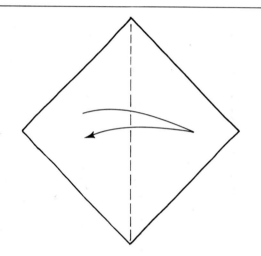

1. Fold square from corner to corner. Unfold paper flat.

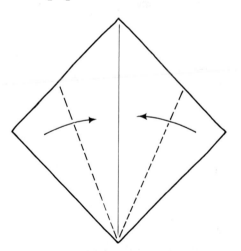

2. Fold two edges to the crease you just made.

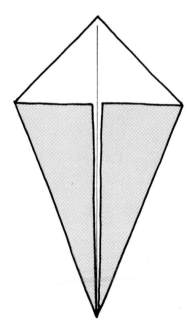

3. Kite Base.

ICE CREAM CONE PARTY INVITATION

Use the Kite Base as an unusual and inexpensive party invitation.

Express your concern for the environment by gluing a green tree to your notes and letters, especially at Christmastime.

YOU NEED

A square of green paper, about 5″ (13 cm)
If paper is colored on one side only, begin with white side up.

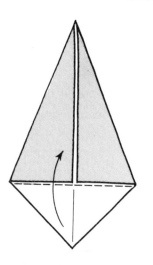

1. Make a Kite Base (page 22). Turn it upside down. Fold the bottom triangle up.

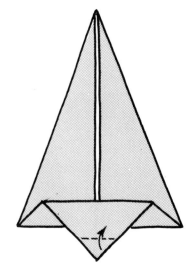

3. Fold tip of corner up.

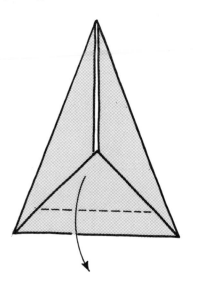

2. Fold corner down.

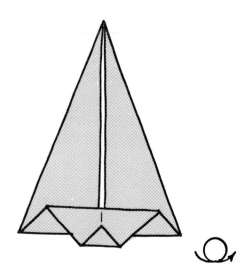

4. Flip paper over from back to front.

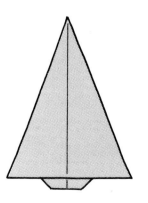

TWO WAYS TO MAKE TREE GREETING CARDS

Write your message on the back of the tree and pop it in an envelope. Or fold a blank piece of paper in half and glue the tree to the front.

5. Tree.

*SANTA CLAUS OR TROLL FINGER PUPPET

Decorate this finger puppet to look like Santa Claus, a Troll, or any other character you like. Make several and wiggle them on your fingers, or use them as Christmas ornaments all through the house. If you cannot get the right kind of paper, use white paper and color one side with a red marker.

YOU NEED

A square of paper, about 5″ (13 cm), red on one side and white on the other

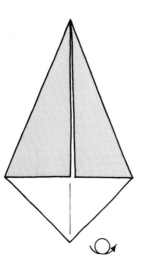

1. Fold a Kite Base (page 22). Turn paper from back to front.

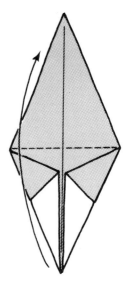

3. Fold bottom corner to top corner.

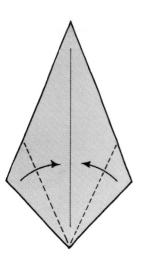

2. Fold short *edges* to the middle.

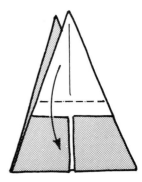

4. Fold down front flap only.

6. Santa Claus or Troll Finger Puppet.

5. Curve paper. Slide one corner in between the two layers on the other corner (or hold together with sticky tape). Twist top corner to look like a tassel.

SANTA CLAUS GREETING CARD

Don't curve the paper (step 5), but leave it flat. Glue on pieces of cotton for beard.

*MASKS

With just a few creases you can fold a Crazy Bird Mask that you can turn into Pinocchio, a spaceman, an insect, and any other fantastic Halloween disguises you choose. Decorate them with kitchen foil, feathers, paper strips, and other additions.

With a few more creases you can create an African Mask. Its contrasting white eyes copy the strong geometric shapes found in ceremonial masks. It's an attractive wall decoration.

You can use construction or any other kind of paper, but for the African Mask use origami, art, or gift wrap paper that is colored on one side only. For a very large mask, you can place two pieces of construction paper in different colors on top of each other and use them as one.

YOU NEED FOR EACH MASK

> A square of paper, about 12″ (30 cm)
> Scissors
> 2 pieces of string, each about 12″ (30 cm) long

CRAZY BIRD MASK

1. Fold a Kite Base (page 22).

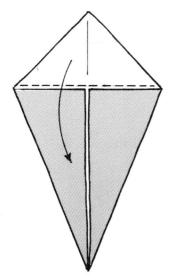

2. Fold the top down.

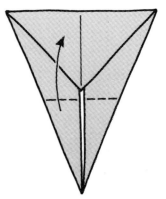

3. Fold the bottom corner up.

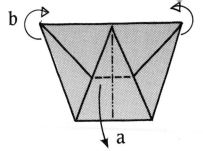

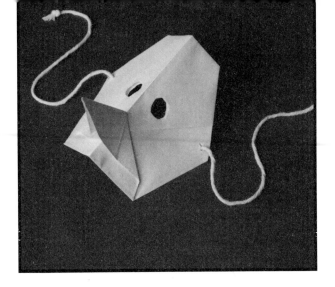

4. (a) Fold the corner down below the bottom edge. (b) Mountain fold paper in half to the back.

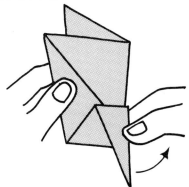

5. Hold at left with one hand. With the other hand pull the nose to the right. Crease sharply at the back of the nose.

6. Cut out holes for eyes.

7. Crazy Bird Mask.

Pierce a hole with the points of the scissors on each side of the mask near the eye holes. Knot string on each side and tie around your head.

PINOCCHIO MASK

1. Fold the Crazy Bird Mask.

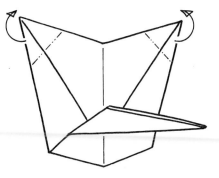

2. Mountain fold the outside corners to the back.

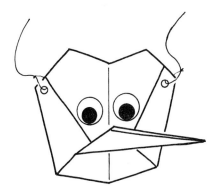

3. Pinocchio Mask.

AFRICAN MASK

1. Fold the Crazy Bird Mask.

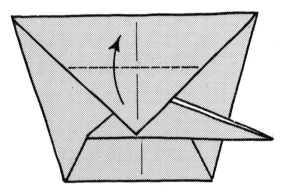

2. Fold up the corner that lies behind the nose.

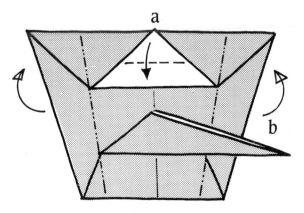

3. (a) Fold it down again. (b) Fold the side edges to the back.

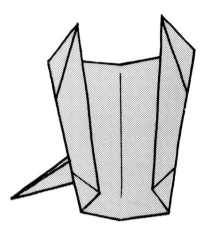

4. Back view.

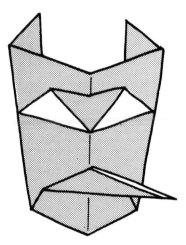

5. African Mask.

For a very large mask you can place two big squares of contruction paper in different colors on top of each other. Use them together as one.

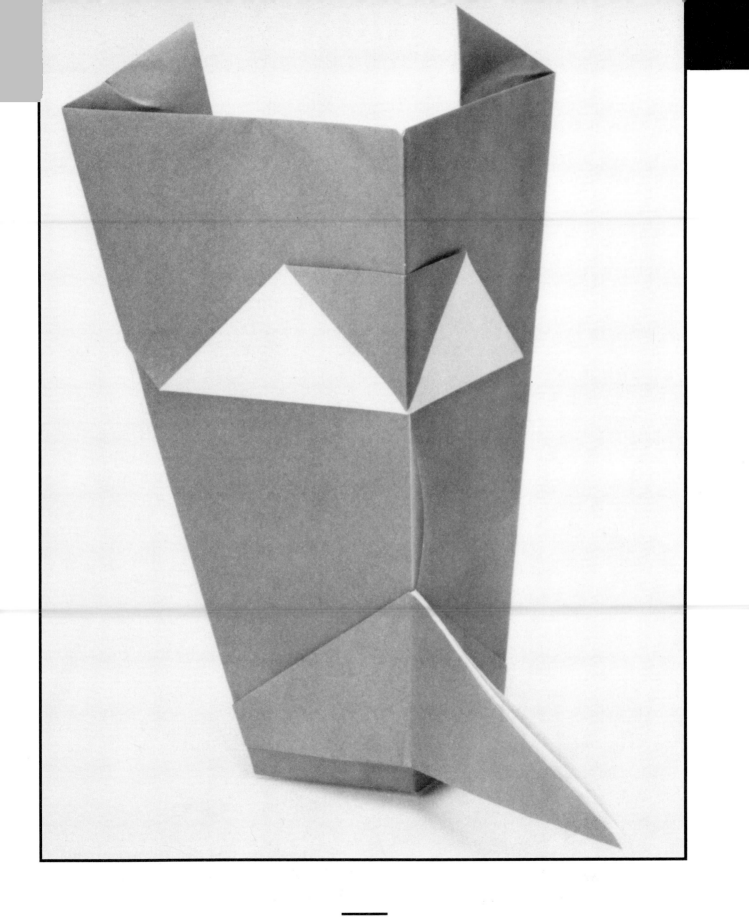

You'll want to make lots of Turkeys for Thanksgiving, but they're fun at any time of the year.

YOU NEED

A square of paper, about 6″ (15 cm), for the turkey
A piece of gift wrap, 3½″ by 10″ (9 cm by 25 cm), for the tail
Stapler
Scissors
If paper is colored on one side only, begin with white side up.

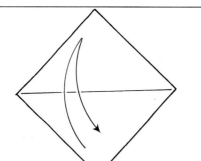

1. Fold the square from corner to corner. Unfold paper flat.

2. Fold two edges to the crease you just made.

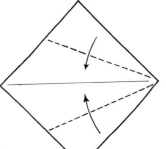

3. Turn the paper over from front to back.

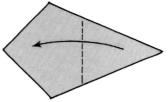

4. Fold the narrow corner to the wider corner.

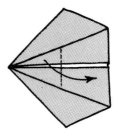

5. Make the head by folding down the tip to the edge.

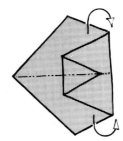

6. Mountain fold the Turkey in half lengthwise, leaving the neck and head showing on the outside.

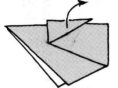

7. Hold the body loosely with one hand. With the other hand pull the neck upright. Crease the front edge to keep it in place.

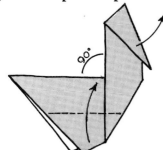

8. Pull the head forward and crease at the back of the head. Fold the bottom up, first on the front and then on the back. This makes a stand.

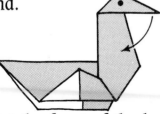

9. Twist the front of the head to point to the body. It looks like a turkey's wattle.

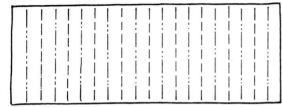

10. Fan pleat the long piece of paper back and forth. Cut a short slit in the middle of the fan. Staple the fan behind the neck of the Turkey, with half of the fan on each side of the body. Open the fan.

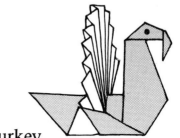

11. Turkey.

TABLE DECORATION

Glue or staple the stand of the Turkey to a cardboard square.

PROUD PEACOCK

Fold the Turkey, but with a smaller head: In step 5, do not fold the corner all the way to the edge. Omit step 9. Make a big tail from a piece of colorful gift wrap, 6″ by 20″ (15 cm by 50 cm). Cut narrow triangles of colored papers and glue them to the head. You can make a very large, dramatic Peacock by using bigger pieces of paper.

33

DINOSAUR (DIAMOND BASE)

YOU NEED

A square of paper, about 8″ (20 cm)
If paper is colored on one side only, begin with white side up.

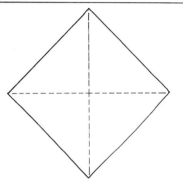

1. Fold corner to corner in both directions. Unfold paper flat each time.

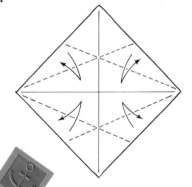

2. Fold the four outside edges to the horizontal crease, one at a time. Unfold the paper flat again each time.

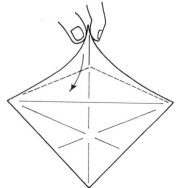

3. Pinch the top corner between your thumb and forefinger and let the paper lie down on the creases made in step 2. Flatten the triangle that you are holding between your fingers to the left. See next drawing. Repeat this with the bottom corner.

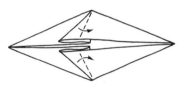

4. Fold as shown. The corners overlap. See next drawing.

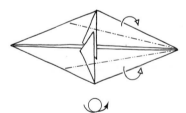

5. Mountain fold two edges to the back. Turn paper over from front to back.

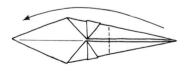

6. Fold the corner of the narrow part to the other end. This will be the neck.

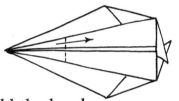

7. Fold the head.

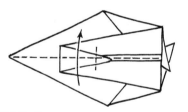

8. (a) Mountain fold the tip of the head. (b) Fold the paper in half, hiding the neck and head inside. Let the legs flip out.

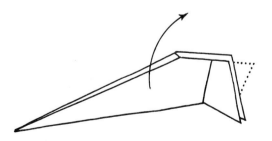

9. Reach inside for the neck and pull it upright. Crease the front sharply to make the neck stay in place.

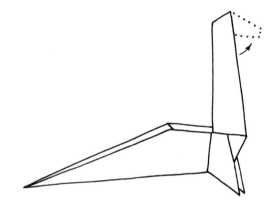

10. Reach inside for the head and pull it out. Crease at the back of the head to make it stay in place.

11. Dinosaur.

In no time flat and for very little cost you can make a big bunch of Heart Valentines or greeting cards for any time of the year. The paper you use has to be red on one side and white on the other. Origami squares or gift wrap are best, but if you can't find them, then combine red construction paper and white stationery. Place them on top of each other and use as one. Always make very sharp creases.

YOU NEED

A square of paper, about 8″ (20 cm), red on one side and white on the other. *Place white side of paper up.*

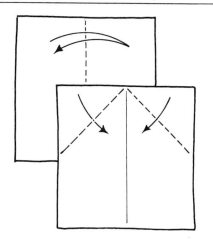

1. Fold paper in half and unfold it. Fold the two top corners to the middle.

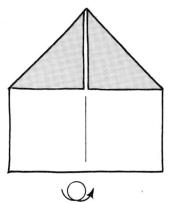

2. Turn the paper over from front to back.

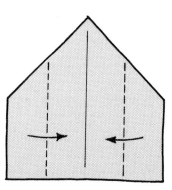

3. Fold the side edges to the middle crease.

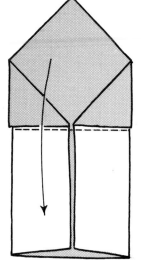

4. Fold the red part down over the white part.

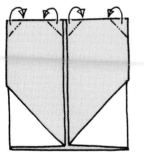

5. Shape the heart by folding the four corners at the top edge to the back.

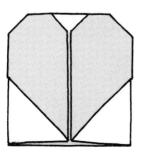

6. Heart Valentine.

BIG HEART

Make a 12″ (30 cm) Heart Valentine from a 24″ (60 cm) paper square.

HEART PIN

Make a 2″ (5 cm) Heart Pin from a 4″ (10 cm) paper square. Cover it with white glue, which dries clear, or clear acrylic spray. Glue on to a brooch pin, which you can buy in craft and bead stores.

**PARTY HAT

Japanese children call this Party Hat a *samurai* (warrior) helmet. It also looks like a Viking helmet. Whatever you decide to call it, it's best to practice folding the hat with paper squares with sides between 6″ and 10″ (15 cm and 25 cm). When you know the steps, make full-size Party Hats to wear from 20″ (50 cm) squares of newspaper or gift wrap.

YOU NEED

A square of paper, about 8″ (20 cm)
If paper is colored on one side only, begin with white side up.

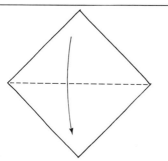

1. Fold top corner to the bottom corner.

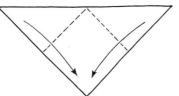

2. Fold both outside corners of the triangle to the bottom corner.

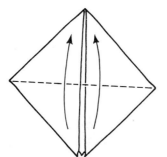

3. Fold the two loose corners to the top.

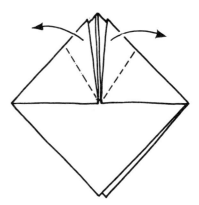

4. Take one of the loose corners and twist it so that it peaks over the edge. Repeat with the other loose corner.

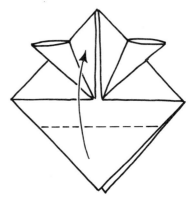

5. Fold the bottom corner up, one layer of paper only.

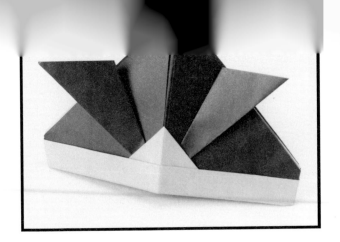

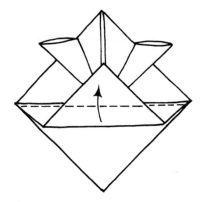

6. Fold paper up again.

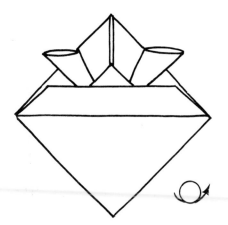

7. Turn paper over.

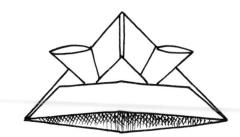

9. Party Hat.

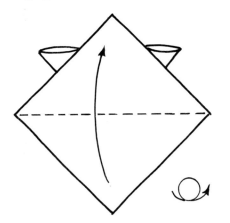

8. Fold bottom corner to top corner.
   Turn paper over.

FIREFIGHTER HELMET

Omit steps 4 and 8.

SIZE ADJUSTMENT

You can make the hat smaller to fit different head sizes. Before step 8, fold in the side corners a little.

**FRIENDLY FROG

The Friendly Frog is an origami favorite. It takes only two minutes to fold, once you know how it works.

YOU NEED

> A 3″ by 5″ (8 cm by 13 cm) index card, or a business card

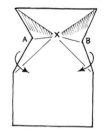

1. Crease an X at the top of the card like this: Fold the short top edge over to the long edge on the left, through the middle of the right corner. Open card flat.

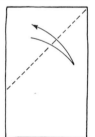

2. Fold the top edge over the long edge on the right, through the middle of the left corner. Open card flat. Here is the X.

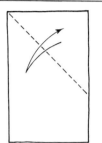

3. Mountain fold to the *back*, right through the middle of the X.

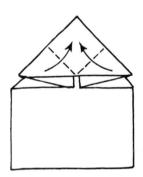

4. Push down at the middle of the X. Bring points A and B to meet together in the middle of the card. Look at the next drawing.

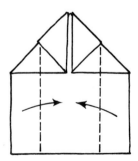

5. Fold the outer corners of the triangle to the top.

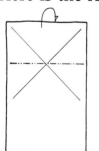

6. Fold the sides to the middle.

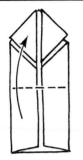

7. Fold the bottom edge to the top.

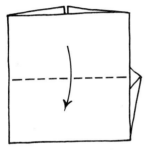

8. Fold the top edge of the front layer to the bottom edge.

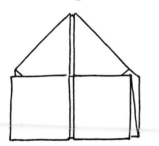

9. Friendly Frog.

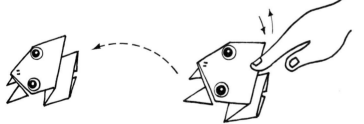

HOW TO MAKE THE FROG JUMP

To give the Friendly Frog power, loosen the front and back legs, so that the Frog is not flat. Tap at the back and the Frog will jump. Sometimes it somersaults.

PARTY GAME

Make the Box on page 50 from a 12″ (30 cm) square of construction paper. Teach party guests to make their own Friendly Frogs. Then have them take turns trying to jump their Frogs into the box. Anyone who lands a Frog in the box gets another turn. Otherwise the next player takes over. The player who lands the Frog most often in the box is the winner.

Invent other rules for the contest.

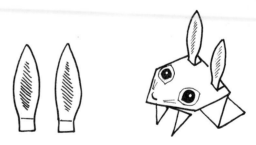

MAGIC HOPPING BUNNY

It's easy to turn the Friendly Frog into a Magic Hopping Bunny. Cut two pink ears and glue or tape them to the Frog. Presto: A Magic Hopping Bunny. Can you make other animals?

*TRIANGLE BASE

The beginning steps for many origamis are the same, and this kind of series is called a Base. Four steps form the Triangle Base, which leads to many other paperfolds. The Star, Flower, Magic Circle, and Ball all begin with the Triangle Base.

YOU NEED

A square of paper, about 6″ (15 cm)
If paper is colored on one side only, begin with colored side up.

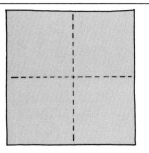

1. Fold a cross on the paper like this: Fold top edge to bottom edge. Open paper flat. Fold the paper in half from side to side. Open paper flat.

2. *Flip over paper from front to back. Very important.*

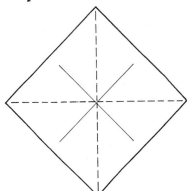

3. Fold the left corner to the right corner. Open paper flat. Fold the top corner to the bottom corner. Do not open the paper.

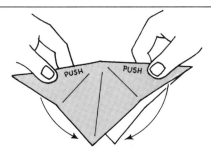

4. Hold the paper exactly as shown with your thumbs and forefingers, and push it into a triangle shape.

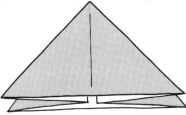

5. Triangle Base.

Buy a roll of gold or silver foil gift wrap paper, and you can make dozens of simple stars for Christmas gifts, package decorations, and tree ornaments.

YOU NEED

A square of foil gift wrap, about 6″ (15 cm)

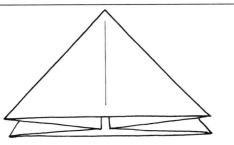

1. Fold square into a Triangle Base (page 42).

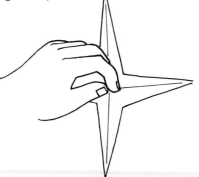

2. Arrange the paper into a star shape. It helps to pinch it at the center.

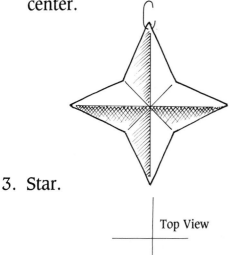

3. Star.

Top View

STARS AND STARS AND STARS

You can vary the size of the star by using smaller or larger squares. For Christmas tree ornaments use 4″ (10 cm) squares. Knot on loops of thread or attach ornament hooks. Stars hold their shapes better when you make them from double layers of paper. For a mobile, combine stars in different sizes and colors.

SPINNING TOY

Place a Star sideways on the point of a pencil. Blow on it to spin it.

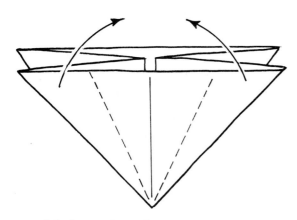

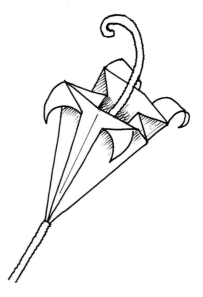

1. Fold the Triangle Base (page 42). On the front, fold outer *edges* to the middle crease. Turn the paper over and repeat on the back.

3. For the stem, curl one end of the pipe cleaner. Pierce a tiny hole in the bottom of the flower. Insert the stem from the top.

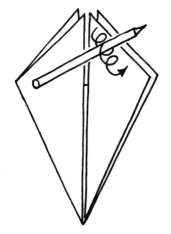

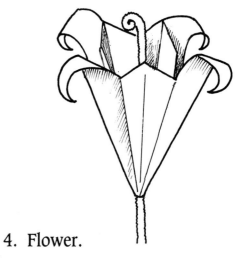

2. Curl the four points at the top over a toothpick. Poke your finger inside and spread the flower open.

4. Flower.

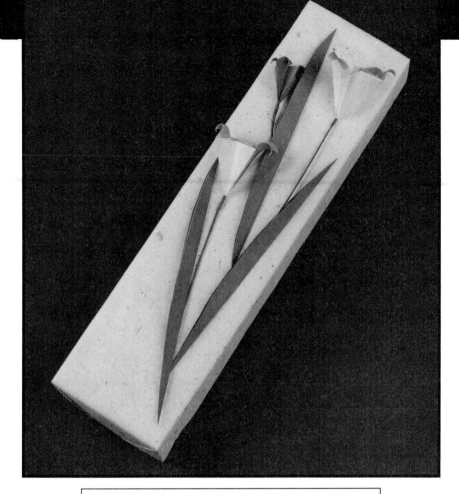

LEAVES

Make leaves from long rectangles of green paper. Fold the paper in half and cut a curved line.

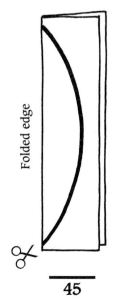

Folded edge

***MAGIC CIRCLE

The Magic Circle is an amazing toy that turns itself inside out. One minute it's a spiky circle and the next minute it looks like a solid wheel. You fold eight paper squares into look-alikes and fit them together. Origami squares or sheets from square memo pads, in two or more colors, are best.

You can fold Magic Circles as surprise party favors. Prepare them ahead of time. Or why not give paper squares to your guests and show them how to make their own Magic Circles?

The Magic Circle is a good example of Unit Origami (also called Modular Origami). Instead of using only a single piece of paper, several squares are combined into boxes, mobiles, and other forms like the Magic Circle. More and more paperfolders enjoy this form of origami.

YOU NEED

8 squares of origami paper, about 4″ (10 cm)
Fold all eight squares in the same way.

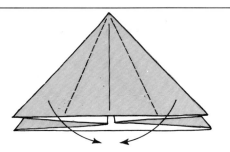

1. Fold the Triangle Base (page 42). Front flaps only, fold outer edges to the middle crease. Turn paper over and repeat on the back.

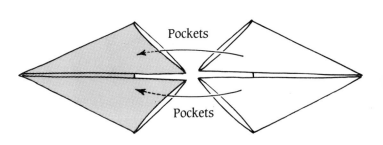

3. Combine two units. Place two units facing each other. Slide the points of the right unit into the "pockets" of the left unit.

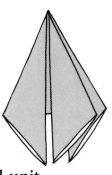

2. Completed unit.

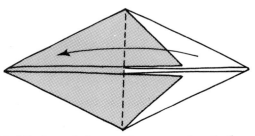

4. Fold the right unit over the left unit.

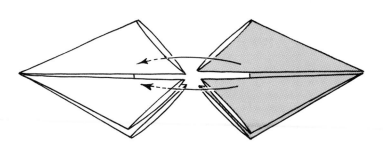

5. Add on the other units, one at a time, by repeating steps 3 and 4. Form them into a circle by joining unit 8 to unit 1.

6. Magic Circle.

Side view of two units

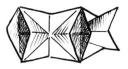

HOW TO CHANGE THE MAGIC CIRCLE

Press the outside of two opposite units to the back and swing them to the middle until the Magic Circle pops into a wheel. Turn it back into a Magic Circle by pressing down in the center of the wheel.

UFO FLOWER

It's a UFO! It's a space station! It's a flower! Flex the Magic Circle halfway and it looks like something from outer space, which you can hang as a mobile. Or turn it into a flower by keeping the sections together with a little glue. For a stem, insert a piece of floral wire down the middle. Hook it over the top, and bend it a little at the bottom of the flower.

The Ball is one of the best-known traditional origamis. Nobody knows when it was invented, but it was a long time ago.

YOU NEED

A square of paper, about 8″ (20 cm)

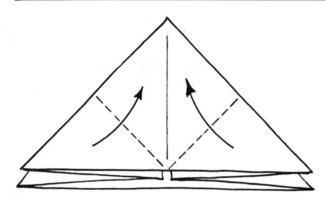

1. Begin with the Triangle Base (page 42). On the front flaps only, fold the outside corners of the triangle up to the top corner. Flip the paper over and repeat the same on the back.

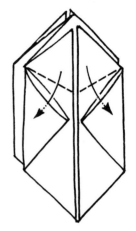

3. With the last step you made little pockets. Slide the loose points at the top into the pockets as far as you can. Repeat on the back.

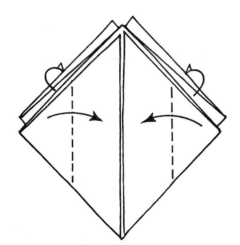

2. On the front flap only, fold the outside corners to the middle. Repeat on the back.

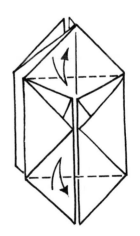

4. Fold back and forth on the broken lines. The Ball looks the same as before, but the lines help to give a better shape to the Ball later on.

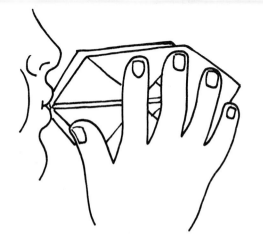

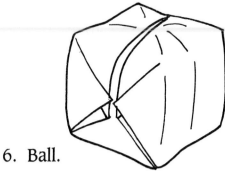

6. Ball.

TREE ORNAMENT

5. Place the Ball lightly between both hands. Blow into the hole that is at one end of the Ball.

You can decorate a whole Christmas tree with paper Balls, small and large, in many colors. Flatten them and store them in a box for next year.

Everyone needs boxes for keeping junk, wrapping gifts, or getting organized. You can make a Box just by folding a piece of paper. If you want a big Box, begin with a big rectangular piece of paper. If you want a mini Box, begin with a tiny rectangular piece of paper. Use construction paper, gift wrap, stationery, or the cover from an old magazine.

YOU NEED

A rectangle of construction paper 9″ by 12″ (23 cm by 30 cm)

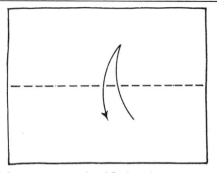

1. Fold paper in half the long way. Unfold.

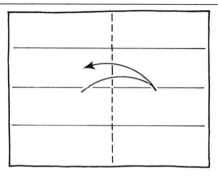

4. Fold the paper in half the short way. Unfold.

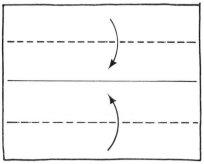

2. Fold the two long edges to the crease you just made.

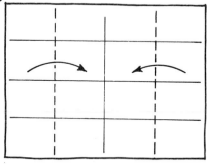

5. Fold the two short edges to the middle. Do not unfold.

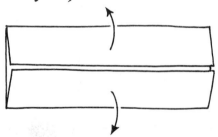

3. Unfold the paper flat.

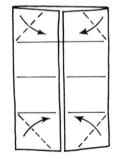

6. Look at your paper and see that the two raw edges are in the middle. Three creases go across. Fold in each of the four corners to line up with the first crease that goes across—not all the way to the middle.

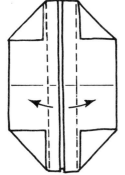

7. Strips of paper in the middle of the paper will not be covered by the corners. Fold the two strips of paper back to hold down the four corners. See next drawing.

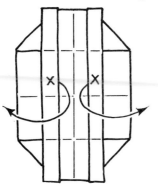

8. Now you have finished all the folding and the next step is magic: Put your hands behind the strips at the X's. Gently pull your hands away from each other.

9. Your Junk Box is complete. Make it boxier by sharpening the creases at the corners and the bottom of the Box.

COVERED BOX

You can make a Covered Box from construction paper, stationery, or other paper. Fold two pieces of paper in the same way. The piece for the bottom of the Box should be about 1/4" (1/2 cm) shorter and narrower than the one for the lid.

BASKET

You can turn your Junk Box into a Basket simply by stapling on a strip of paper for a handle.
   Here are some useful ideas:
- For Easter, make Baskets from pastel-colored paper.
- For a party, make a Basket for each guest from paper 4" by 5" (10 cm by 13 cm).
- Make a Basket using a double layer of beautiful gift wrap. It can be filled with small things and kept on a table or dresser.

*AIRPLANE

Everyone loves to fly paper airplanes, and dozens of different kinds have been invented by kids and adults. The one shown here may be new to you. After you have folded it, why don't you try to design your own new pattern for "flying wings."

YOU NEED

A sheet of notebook paper, 8½″ by 11″ (22 cm by 28 cm)

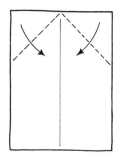

1. Fold paper in half. Unfold.

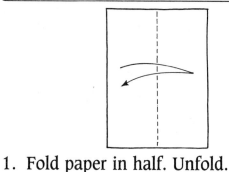

2. Fold two corners to the crease.

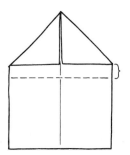

3. Fold top down. Crease is about 1″ (3 cm) from the triangle.

4. Fold two corners to the middle.

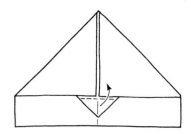

5. Fold up small triangle.

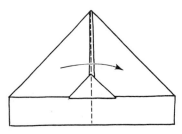

6. Fold plane in half.

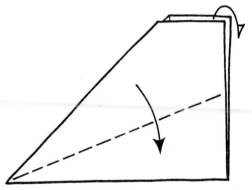

7. Fold wings down, first on the front and then on the back.

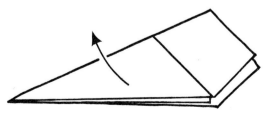

8. Loosen the wings to be at right angles to the body. Pitch the plane in an upward curve.

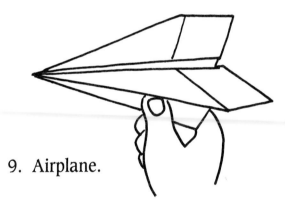

9. Airplane.

EXPERIMENTS

Small variations sometimes help improve the aerodynamics of flight patterns. Try curving the wings, attaching a paper clip to the nose, or experimenting in other ways. Bend up the ends of the wings (where the paper is a single layer), and it may loop back to you.

The beginning steps for many origamis are the same. This kind of series is called a Base. It's a good idea to practice and remember how to make the Square Base because it leads to many, many things.

YOU NEED

A square of paper, about 6" (15 cm). If paper is colored on one side only, begin with colored side up.

1. Crease an X on the square like this: Fold corner to corner. Open the paper flat. Fold the other two corners together. Open the paper flat.

2. Flip the paper over from front to back. *Very important.*

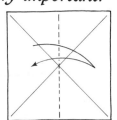

3. Fold the paper in half from side to side. Open paper flat.

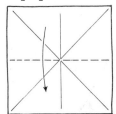

4. Fold the top edge to the bottom edge. Do not open.

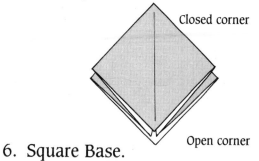

5. Hold at the folded edge with both hands exactly as shown. Move your hands to each other until the paper forms a square. Put it flat on the table. Two flaps must be on each side. If you have only one flap on one side and three on the other, then flip one over.

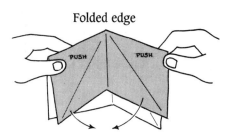

6. Square Base.

54

*PUPPET

YOU NEED

A square of paper, about 6″ (15 cm)

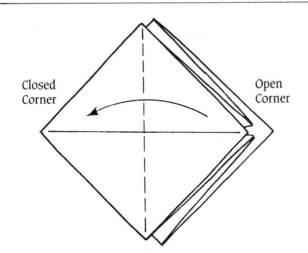

Closed
Corner

Open
Corner

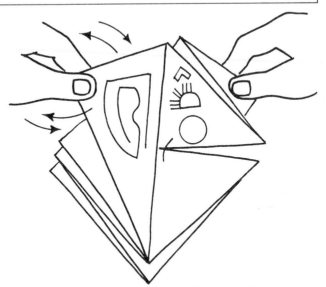

1. Fold a Square Base (page 54).
Place it sideways. On the front and
the back fold the loose layers to
the closed corner.

2. Puppet. Draw on a face and ears.
Hold the ears with both hands.
Move them back and forth to let
the puppet "talk."

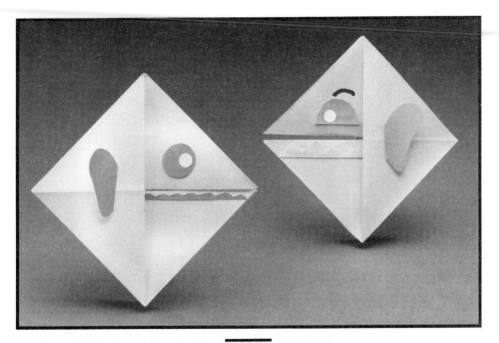

*SAILBOAT

YOU NEED

A square of paper, about 6″ (15 cm)
If paper is colored on one side only, begin with the white side up.

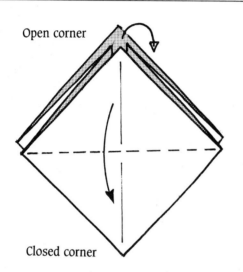

Open corner

Closed corner

1. Fold a Square Base (page 54).
   Place it with the closed corner
   down. On the front and the back,
   fold the loose layers down.

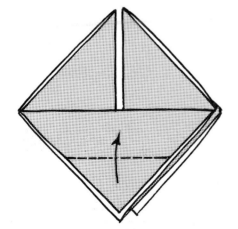

2. Fold all layers of the bottom corner
   to the middle. This makes a stand.

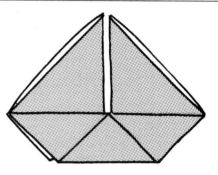

3. Turn boat back to front.

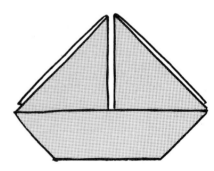

4. Sailboat.

VARY THE SAILBOAT

You can make one sail smaller than
the other: Fold one sail down over the
boat. Fold it up again forming a pleat.
Tuck the bottom of the sail inside the
boat.

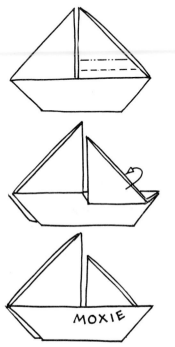

NAME TAGS AND PLACE CARDS

The front of the Sailboat has a perfect space for writing on names.

POP-UP GREETING CARD

Glue the *stand only* of a Sailboat to a card. Write your greeting on the card, and slide it into an envelope. When your friend takes out the card, the Sailboat pops up.

*HELICOPTER

The Helicopter flies best when made from an origami square or other lightweight paper. Otherwise it will not twirl, but drop straight down.

YOU NEED

A square of paper, about 6″ (15 cm)

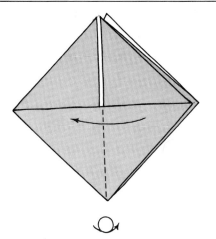

1. Fold the Sailboat (drawing 2, page 56). Fold the flap on the right over to the left, like a page of a book. Flip the paper over sideways and repeat on the back, again folding from the right to the left.

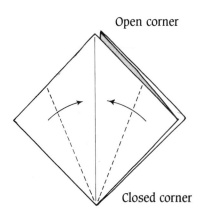

Open corner

Closed corner

2. Front flaps only, fold the edges to the middle. Flip the paper over and repeat on the back.

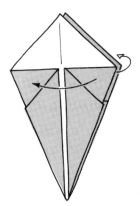

3. Fold the flap on the right over to the left, like a page of a book. Flip the paper over and repeat on the back.

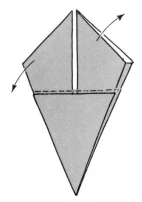

4. Bend one helicopter blade to the front and the other to the back.

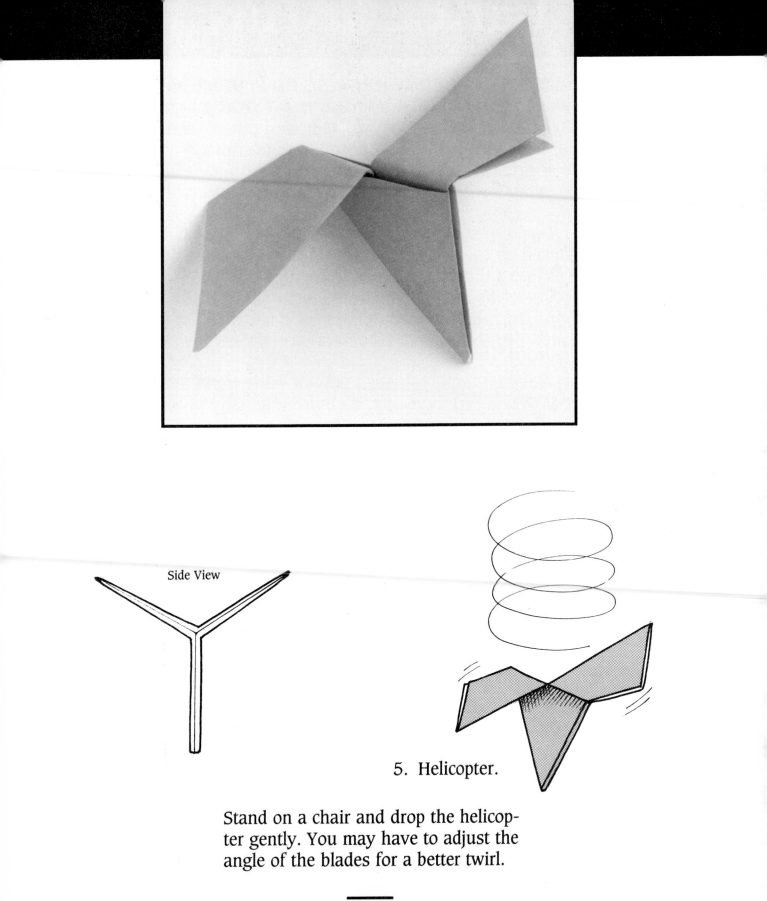

Side View

5. Helicopter.

Stand on a chair and drop the helicopter gently. You may have to adjust the angle of the blades for a better twirl.

***INTERNATIONAL PEACE CRANE

The International Peace Crane represents the hope for peace all over the world. The crane is a bird that may live as long as a thousand years. For this reason, in Japan and other Asian countries, it has become a symbol for long life. The crane is not only a very popular origami, but often appears in paintings. It became a worldwide symbol when the story of Sadako Sasaki became known.

Sadako Sasaki died at the age of twelve, a victim of radiation disease caused by the atom bomb that fell on Hiroshima in 1945. She tried to fold a thousand cranes in the age-old belief that she would recover if she accomplished this task. Sadly, she could only complete 644, but she inspired millions of children all over the world to send paper cranes to Hiroshima to express their own hope for peace.

You can make origami cranes as gifts or hang them as mobiles. The crane is now a rare bird that is environmentally protected.

YOU NEED

A square of paper, about 8″ (20 cm)

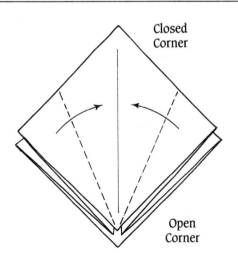

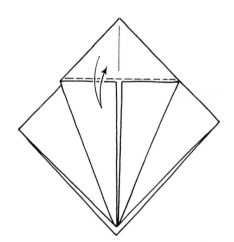

1. Fold a Square Base (page 54). Place closed corner away from you. Fold the outer edges on the front flaps to the middle crease. Turn the paper over and repeat this with the two flaps on the back.

2. Draw a pencil (or imaginary) line between the ends of the creases. Fold back and forth on that line. Paper looks as before, but the crease helps you with the next step.

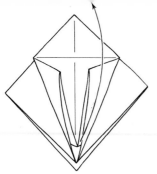

3. (a) Pop the two front flaps apart. Find the loose corner at the bottom. Lift it up in the direction of the arrow.

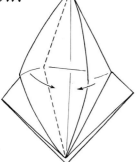

(b) Bring the outside edges of the paper to the middle and flatten it into a long diamond. The trick is to keep the crease made in step 2. Turn the paper over and repeat on the back.

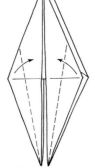

4. This diamond shape is called the Bird Base. It has two "legs" at the bottom. Fold their outer edges to the middle, first on the front flaps. Turn the paper over and repeat on the back.

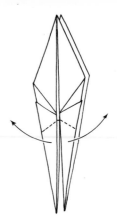

5. Make the neck and tail by folding the "legs" to the outside.

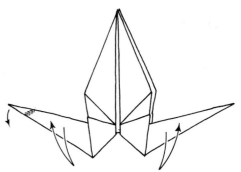

6. Fold the "legs" down again. Then fold them up on the creases made in step 5, but this time in between the two main layers of paper. Fold the head down in between the two main layers of the neck.

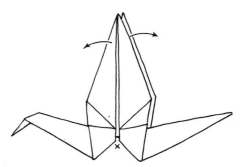

7. Inflate the crane by holding a wing in each hand. Pull your hands apart gently and at the same time blow into the opening at point X.

8. International Peace Crane.

MOBILE

Attach a string or length of fishing line to a big crane made from a 15" (40 cm) paper square and hang it as a mobile. It's a lovely baby gift when you use pastel colors.

HOW TO SEND INTERNATIONAL PEACE CRANES

Cranes are usually sent flat to Hiroshima. That is also the way they are strung together, whether into the enormous construction of a "Thousand Cranes" or a lesser number. You can send Peace Cranes in the mail as greetings for birthdays and other occasions. Mention the goodwill and environmental meaning of your gift.

***FLAPPING BIRD

The Flapping Bird has a surprise ending that's quite amazing: It flaps its wings up and down. It is folded in almost the same way as the International Peace Crane.

YOU NEED

A square of paper, about 8″ (20 cm)

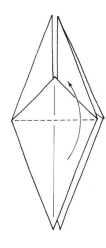

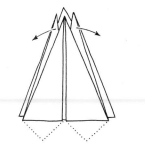

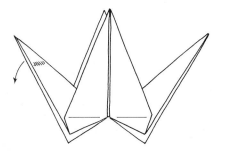

1. Follow the directions for the International Peace Crane (page 60), but leave out step 4, which makes the "legs" narrower.

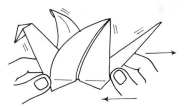

2. At the end do not inflate the bird. Make the wings flap like this: Hold the bird with one hand, and gently pull the tail back and forth with the other hand. (Do not pull it up and down.)

TIP:
If the wings don't flap, then reach inside between the wing and the body and wiggle the wing. Do it on both sides.

ACKNOWLEDGMENTS AND CREDITS

Origami Magic contains designs that may be centuries old, and new ones I created especially for this book. The *Helicopter* was designed by Robert Abes, the *Heart Valentine* by Francis Ow, and the *Magic Circle* that turns into the *Star Wheel* by a Japanese paperfolder. I thank them, and Yoli and Tyler Anyon; Janet, Dennis, David, Perri, and Rachel Temko; Brentin Williams; and participants in my origami classes at the San Diego Museum of Art for testing the instructions. I also thank Joyce Rockmore for going over the manuscript; V'Ann Cornelius, Cath Kachur, Mark Kennedy, Jeanne Lynch, Merida, Barbara Murphy, Michael Shall, and especially Henry Petzal for their support; and many other paperfolder friends.

ABOUT THE AUTHOR

Florence Temko loves origami and for many years has shared the fun through programs in schools, colleges, libraries, and museums. She is the author of thirty how-to books on various crafts, including three for Scholastic: *Paper Capers* (1974), *Paper Tricks* (1988), and *Paper Tricks II* (1990).